I Think I'm Happier Than I Think I Am

... A Pastor's Thoughts

By Reverend James O'Leary

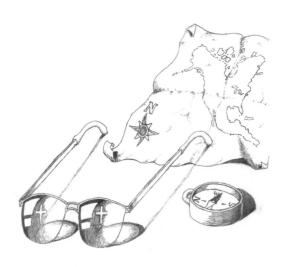

Battle Creek Area Catholic Schools 2002

Editor, Kathleen Toth
Title page illustration by Sean Miller
Cover photograph by Kathleen Toth and Suzanne Bauman
Printed in the United States of America
First Edition

Copyright © 2002 Published by:

Battle Creek Area Catholic Schools
63 North 24th Street
Battle Creek, Michigan 49015

ISBN 0-9726194-0-2

The Glory of God is the human person fully alive.

And how do we get there?
How do we become fully alive?

One day at a time-in Prayer.

To all those who reach for life-and keep reaching.

Jim O'Leary

"**I** THINK I AM HAPPIER THAN I THINK I AM." For years, our diocese was blessed with a special priest, the Reverend Monsignor Joseph Bryne. He was loving, charming and witty. He was an intellectual. He learned to read Russian in his 60's so that he could read the novels of Dostoevsky. I hate such people! Fr. Byrne had a way of dropping an enigmatic statement on his friends, which left them shaking their heads. He dropped the above statement on a bunch of priests. "I think I am happier than I think I am." What is he talking about?

Joe Byrne went on to explain what he meant. He pointed out that where we focus our attention would largely determine whether we are happy or miserable. We have a strong inclination to live on the surface of life. That is where the big ups and downs exist. If I spend my time on the surface of life, I will have lots of worries, lots of anxieties and lots of anger. If I live on the surface of life, I keep focused on disagreeable people, frustrating situations. It is not hard to be unhappy on the surface of life.

However, I have other options as to where I spend my time. I can go deeper into myself and see life from that viewpoint. I can reach a level of myself where I am most forgiving, most loving. The ups and downs of life look different from that viewpoint. I can reach the deepest part of myself where God resides. From there, everything looks different.

And then, according to Joe Byrne, I find, "I think I am happier than I think I am."

SOME PEOPLE HAVE SUGGESTED that the bulletin should have some reflections from the pastor. I agree. So, here goes.

I have been in Battle Creek and in St. Joseph Parish for one month. I have had some first impressions.

I immediately noticed a very impressive parish plant. The grounds and buildings are in wonderful shape. People obviously take pride in their parish. There is a playground over in the corner that looks more like Walt Disney World. I was impressed.

Battle Creek has been for me a delightful surprise. I knew nothing of Battle Creek. All I knew is that whenever I came here, I got lost. My impression was that Battle Creek was like Gary, Indiana, with corn flakes. A very wrong impression! Battle Creek, I find, is a beautiful, alive city. I enjoy being here. I will enjoy being here. And I have not been lost yet.

Lastly, the people of St. Joseph have been overwhelmingly gracious to me. I have never received a more loving welcome. I do appreciate your kindness to me. I very much look forward to being the pastor of this group of people. Together we can make the experience of church enjoyable and enriching. I am so happy to be with you.

N EW BEGINNINGS are gifts from God, but they do not always seem like gifts. Every time we "start over," we make a painful adjustment. I have watched so many older people go through the agonizing experience of losing a spouse. What a new beginning that is. After decades of marriage, people have to be alone in the house. They must eat meals alone day after day. This is truly starting your life all over again. People are often called upon to do this in their 70's and 80's. I watched my own father go through this new beginning. It was terrible. He did not think of this loss as a gift at first. But he made the adjustment and ended up all the stronger for it. He was able to enjoy his remaining years.

Most of our new beginnings are not so painful or traumatic. Most of us had a new beginning last week: school started. This obviously affects the students and teachers. It affects most of our families. Most parents do not find this new beginning troublesome. The beginning of school has a huge effect upon me as a priest. For so many of us, summertime is truly a different schedule. It may not be vacation time, but it is more relaxed.

Whenever we have a new beginning, we have an opportunity to change. God uses new beginnings to bring us down the road closer to Himself. In this new beginning, we all can become better at what we do. I tell priests who are changing parishes that we need to change more than our address. We are "beginning," starting over. We can become whatever we want. It is "opportunity" time.

So, happy new beginning. Use it well.

S INCE I ARRIVED at St. Joseph Parish, people have been asking if I am feeling at home. The question makes me evaluate what it means to be "at home."

Within a few days, I was answering the question, "Yes, I feel much at home in the rectory." But how could I be at home that quickly? Being at home has to mean more than just unpacking. Then I realized that I had never really felt at home in my previous residence, even after 10 years. I am already forgetting where some of the rooms were located. I am beginning to realize that the last time I felt at home in a place, was in the big white house on Chestnut Street in Lansing. That was my family home where I was raised. I realize that "home" for me is no longer a place.

There are situations in which I feel at home. When I am around friends and loved ones, I feel at home, wherever we are. I left loved ones in Coldwater, and I do not feel at home without them. So, to get back to the original question, "Do I feel at home at St. Joseph?" The answer is yes, if we are speaking of the rectory. But the answer is no, if we are speaking of people. There is no such thing as instant friendship, instant intimacy. But this is changing fast; I am well on the way to feeling at home among the people of St. Joseph Parish.

So, home will never be a place for me again. Home is where loved ones are. Eventually, we will all find out that home is where the Ultimate Loved One is. This was all stated very simply by someone who said, "Home is where the heart is." He was not whistling "Dixie."

T HE PRIMARY CALL of a Christian is the call to conversion, or change of life. The constant message of St. John the Baptist and Jesus was a call to conversion. "Change your life. The Kingdom of God is at hand." This call still applies to us. Today, as in every age, some are in need of drastic conversion. Some only need smaller conversion. But we all need some conversion, some change of life. This is an inherent part of following Jesus.

I remember giving a retreat when we were discussing change and someone said, "What if you do not really need to change?" This is a misunderstanding of Jesus' teaching. No one can make such a statement unless they are already perfect, as God is perfect. In history, the ones who felt the most need to change were our greatest saints. They, above all people, were aware of their shortcomings.

Yet we all implicitly make this statement our own. If someone asked, "Do you need to change?" we would readily agree to that need. But if they then ask, "What do you need to change?" we might be stumped. Change in general? Yes! Specific change? Forget it! If I need to change, I must keep in mind the "what" and the "how." What do I need to change, and how do I get there?

I GUESS YOU COULD call this a "What I did on my summer vacation" column. I had occasion during July to go to Denver. I was meeting some friends to help them drive across the country to Michigan. Problem? I had to figure out how to get to Denver without a car. Last-minute plane reservations were outrageously expensive. The train was all booked up. Solution? I took a bus!

I had not been on a long bus trip in many years. I presumed that bus travel had become more comfortable over the years. I was wrong! With all due respect to Greyhound and Indian Trails, the bus trip was a horror. The seats were cramped and uncomfortable. It was difficult to sleep, even to read. The bus was packed. The temperature seemed always too hot or too cold. The bus terminals along the way were dreadful. The best one I saw was in Battle Creek. This is rough traveling. Yet, I had a ball.

When the crowd is right, nothing else matters that much. The people on that bus were a delightful, somewhat crazy crowd. People were either poor or cheap. I do believe I exhausted the second category all by myself. Some white people, some black people, some Hispanic, tons of little kids, one young man from Italy, and a well-disguised priest. The young Italian was so hungry to hear Italian; I gave him all I had. He stuck with me for five hundred miles.

All these people were uncomfortable, but they seemed to pull together. To say we became family would be to exaggerate, but we did pull together. Mothers with little ones got help from those nearby. One large man was so uncomfortable, the whole bus conspired to get him a double seat. We all learned to care about each other. The whole trip was quite an experience. When the crowd is right, nothing else matters.

HAVE YOU EVER NOTICED how many people identify themselves as perfectionists? Everywhere you hear people saying, "Well, the trouble with me is that I am a perfectionist." It makes one wonder. If you read the paper, you find corruption, violence on our streets, in our families, violence toward women, toward children, stealing, lying, murder, and just plain, nasty conduct. So how can we have such a crummy world that is peopled almost exclusively by perfectionists? It is a mystery!

Well, there are perfectionists... and perfectionists. People declare themselves to be a perfectionist if they experience acute pain from: a spot on the hood of their car, three dandelions in the front yard, a baby crying in church, the guy ahead driving too slowly, a spouse putting the paper towel roll on backwards (or forwards, or upside-down). One has to wonder what these things have to do with perfection. I do believe that they have nothing to do with real perfection. However, I find it rather comforting to say, "Well, the trouble with me is that I am a perfectionist." It is so much better than saying, "Well, the trouble with me is that I am a neurotic fuss pot." Too many of my friends would readily agree. There is no fun in that. I would rather be a "perfectionist."

Jesus said much about perfection. Perfection means loving, sensitivity and service. According to Jesus, perfection is not an obsession with the details of human living. There is an easy test. If your form of perfectionism makes you a pleasure to be around, it is "the real thing." If it drives your loved ones crazy, your "perfectionism" has nothing to do with perfection.

Let us be real.

OUR YOUTH GROUP BEGAN meeting last Sunday night. Their discussion started out with a quote from Henry David Thoreau. That is a very good way to begin. Thoreau is one of our fine men of letters, and certainly, one of our most precious thinkers.

Thoreau said, "I have great faith in a seed. Show me where you have a seed, and I am prepared to expect wonders."

This time of year we are surrounded by children at St. Joseph. Our school started a few weeks ago. Our religious program for our public school students began last Sunday. So did our youth group. We have kids of every age around. Each one of them represents a seed, a wonderful seed. A seed is power; a seed is potential. Each one of our children is all that potential and power. But, like a seed, it has to be nourished and cared for. It is so wonderful to see that potential in a child and to see it develop.

I looked around our youth group last Sunday, and I saw more than seeds. I saw people on the verge of adulthood. There is potential here, but there is actuality too. These teenagers are well on their way. They are fun to be with. In families, in religion classes, in school, we try so hard to instill our Christian values. I see so much in our young people to be hopeful about.

I suspect that none of you needs a 60-year-old bachelor to tell you how precious children are, especially your own children. For all of our teachers, I can say thank you for sharing your children with us. We try to benefit them. They in turn, help us. They certainly give us joy. "Show me where you have a seed, and I am prepared to expect wonders." Henry David, you said it.

E VEN BEFORE CHRIST, there existed a wonderful philosophy in Greece and Rome. The ancient Romans were practical people. They did not ask themselves theoretical questions. They asked how they, as people, could become happy. They concluded that they must keep the source of happiness within themselves. They were the Stoic Philosophers. The writer Epictetus and the Emperor Marcus Aurelius were of their company. They were wise and wonderful.

The Stoics believed that they could not depend on the "outside" for happiness. The "outside" is beyond my control. I must keep some control over my happiness or I will always be a victim. Example: I would be happy if my wife (husband) were cheerful in the morning. I will be happy when I win the lottery. This is not the road to happiness. Happiness is securely found only from within.

The Stoics said that we could not let our desires go unrestrained. If I let my desires go wild, I can convince myself that I need a yacht to be happy. I do not need a yacht, or a VCR, or a Porsche, or a TV. We can decide what we need; we can be content with what we have. In this regard, there are two ways to get rich. I define a rich person as one who earns more than he wants to spend. You could earn a fortune, more than you could ever want to spend. Or you could limit your desire to spend. J.P. Morgan chose the first way; Francis of Assisi chose the second. They were both rich.

The Stoics were a secular philosophy. They did not bring God into the picture. When we Christians take the Stoic wisdom and add our spirituality, then we really have a plan of life. Look inside yourself for happiness. Inside you find the God who loves you. This God is the only sure source of happiness. Now we find that Francis of Assisi just might have been the happiest individual whoever lived.

T HIS SUMMER I ATTENDED a wedding performed by an old friend, Fr. Ed Prus. It was a special wedding. He is a special priest. I had not seen him in 30 years. I expected that he would have evolved into a piece of work. He has. The wedding was unique.

At this wedding, the priest gave a gift to the bride and groom during the ceremony. Different! In fact, he had four packages wrapped for them, but they had to choose one and leave the other three. As they chose, and unwrapped their present, Fr. Prus pointed out that we all have to make choices in life. We must be careful to make good choices and then treasure them and be happy with them. We cannot be dreaming about the choices not taken. Those choices may be attractive, even better than our choice. However, we must make choices and commitments. If our choices are good, we must treasure them, and not worry about the "roads not taken." I cannot be happy in life if I am constantly thinking, "Gosh, I could have had a V8."

My friend made the point at the wedding that they had chosen each other and should treasure each other and not keep thinking of the other options. He put the remaining three presents away. The bride and groom did not get to see them. They had made their choice. It is my guess that every time they look at the beautiful piece of art that was their gift, they will remember about making choices and sticking with those choices.

No one gets all the "goodies" in life. We must choose. So, may our choices be wise and may we remain happy with those choices. That is not a wish; it must be a resolution. We cannot wait to be happy with our choices. We must work to be happy with our choices.

After performing about 800 weddings, I received a lesson in weddings from my friend, Ed Prus. For that, he has my thanks. He is quite a fellow.

EVERYONE IS SAYING, "Where did the summer go? It went so fast. Now it is gone." This makes me think about time and how we use time. Wasting time has always been frowned upon. Wasting time means passing time unproductively. How silly! Some of the best times of my life were not productive in any real sense. They were just wonderful. They produced nothing but joy. The Trappist monk, Fr. Matthew Kelty, even calls prayer a conscientious waste of time.

I think abusing time means forgetting that it is a gift. To go through a day without enjoying is wasting time. I say, "Where has summer gone?" but it is right outside the door. It is a beautiful day today. If there is only one day left of summer, it is worth enjoying. In years gone by, I used to celebrate Mass in a men's prison. Naturally, the men were dreaming of the day when they would get out. Then, they would be happy. I used to say, "Unless you find a way to be happy today, maybe you are never going to be happy." That would make them very angry. How could anyone be happy in a prison? Yet some were! How could anyone be happy anywhere? It is a rough world. People are happy when they decide to be happy.

We are inclined to wait until the world becomes perfect so that we can be happy. We waste a lot of time; we wait forever. We have to find a way to be happy, to enjoy, in an imperfect world. The only way to waste time really is to spend time without joy. So, enjoy the last days of summer. Summer is not gone. It is here. Do not be productive, but do not waste time. Enjoy!

T HERE IS A BASIC mystery about every human person. I think that the mystery has to do with how God loves us. That, we cannot know; we cannot evaluate. The love God has for a person gives that person great potential. There is the mystery. A few people know who I am. Only God knows who I could be.

We all need to think about our possibilities. With the Grace of God, so much is possible for each one of us. Jesus said, "Be perfect as your Heavenly Father is perfect." Can we do that? I doubt it. But we can come closer than we think, in a lifetime.

I believe there is a principle behind our thinking of our own possibilities. The principle is: What another person can do, I can do. Keeping this principle in mind, we look at others.

For example: The white clad figure of Pope John Paul II in a prison cell leaning forward, head to head with the Turkish assassin who tried to kill him. In the past generation, I cannot think of a more powerful image of forgiveness. I suspect that nothing a Pope could do could change the world as much as that sincere, public act of forgiveness.

For example: The Vatican asked Father James Murray to be the Bishop of Kalamazoo at age 65. As he was preparing in his own mind for retirement, the call comes to begin a whole new career. He said "yes."

For example: I have a friend who just finished her last chemotherapy treatment. Her recent statement, "I have been doing a dance with cancer. It has brought more joy into my life than anything I have ever experienced."

God gave us incredible potential. We need to think about our possibilities, remembering the principle, "What another person can do, I can do."

"**N**EVER MEASURE the height of a mountain until you have reached the top. Then you will see how low it is." - Dag Hammarskjold

I remember when I started to learn Latin in the seminary. I did fine for three days. On the fourth, the professor came to class and began to speak Latin. He actually expected the students to answer back in Latin. I panicked. It could not be done. Latin was a dead language. No one spoke it. Impossible! However, eight years later, I was sitting in a classroom in Rome listening to a lecture in Latin and responding with ease.

When we are faced with any new challenge, we can so easily lose perspective. Anything new can look impossible. Some things we may face are impossible. But, I think very few. God has given us a glorious capacity to expand ourselves. We have many physical limitations, but our mind can soar. We must push ourselves. We only find out what we can do when we push ourselves or are pushed by others. The difference between a good student and a poor one is often a parent or a teacher who had high expectations of the student and pushed.

I was blessed with parents and teachers like that. I found out that "the impossible" was often do-able. I found out that mountains look a lot higher from the bottom than from the top. The Psalmist says, "What a wonder is man, a little less than the angels."

Let us not sell ourselves short.

I LIKE TO THINK back and recall very special celebrations of the Mass. I can remember some very bad celebrations too, but I do not try to recall them.

A friend and I were traveling in Kentucky. He wanted to visit a friend in a cloistered convent in the area. We went there for Mass. About 12 to 15 nuns attended. The priest, an elderly man, entered and began the prayers of the Mass. I noticed immediately that the entire congregation said all of the prayers of the Mass with the priest. Even the Eucharistic Prayer was recited in common with the priest celebrant. According to my knowledge of liturgical law, this was most improper.

Something else seemed strange. The priest seemed to be about a half a word behind the rest of the congregation. This was maintained throughout. The Mass was, nevertheless, beautifully done, as one would expect in a cloistered convent. Later I was curious about the two peculiarities, and so I asked our nun friend about it.

"Father had a stroke two years ago. He has recovered amazingly, but he still can't say the prayers of the Mass without stammering," she said. "He led us in Liturgy for so many years. Now he is partly disabled, and so we lead him. We think it is fitting."

Indeed! I realized that I had not been at a Mass that was just beautifully done. I had been at a Mass that was unforgettable. The image remains, of the small group of nuns and the old priest helping each other in their journey to the Lord.

CONSIDER THE POSTAGE STAMP: its usefulness consists in its ability to stick to one thing until it gets there. We will not get anywhere without the ability to stick with something. The ability to commit ourselves is a necessity. Our power of committing ourselves is a necessary element in our future happiness.

I think that often people fail because they try to commit themselves to the wrong person or job. There is no particular virtue in clinging to a commitment that is a loser. I certainly know people who have started a profession and then changed because they needed to. They were not fitted for their first profession. I have known people who divorced who needed to. The relationship was dead. The only thing to do with a dead thing is bury it. I have also seen many who made that decision too quickly. I have seen marriages that were dead, come to life. It is a decision of prudence.

Given the right commitment, we must persevere. This is the road to happiness. Real authentic people, people of substance, know how to commit.

I had an English bulldog once. I loved her, even though she was fat, ugly, lazy, disagreeable and stubborn. She drooled too much. However, she did have one redeeming characteristic. When she bit, she never let go. Very nice!

GOD'S M & M'S. A friend was telling me about his family. He says that almost every day, his wife has occasion to give the small children a cup of Cheerios, or Doritos, or some such snack. It helps them keep quiet in places like church. (Our maintenance man reports many Cheerios on the church floor on Monday mornings.) Then, once in a while, Momma puts M & M's in the cup as a special treat. The kids love it.

Then Momma will say, "Please can I have one of your M & M's?" and the child will take one and put it up to his mother's mouth. Then she gets really happy and gives the child a big hug. My friend says they go through this ritual every time the M & M's are brought out. He loves watching the whole routine.

He says, "Why does she ask for an M & M?" She does not need to ask. They come from her. She has a whole bag full in the kitchen. But she says, "They taste so much better as a gift from a child."

My friend says that this reminds him of our giving to God. We only give what God has already given us. All of our M & M's come from Him. But God enjoys receiving some back from His children. And He waits to give us a hug. God enjoys the exchange with His children. That is my friend's interpretation, and I do like it.

We all need to remember that all we give to God comes from Him. We are only giving back a share. I hope we are all generous with our M & M's. We all need the hugs.

I HAVE BEEN THINKING lately of the wonders of humor, of all the times I have gotten upset when I could have simply laughed. Laughing is so much easier on the blood pressure than anger.

I got my formative lesson in laughing from a classmate in 1967. Frank was a priest in a Pennsylvania diocese. We had both been ordained about six years at that time. We were both in very troubled parish assignments. It was a time of renewal and change in the church. We both wanted to bring about renewal and our pastors did not. Our living situations were filled with tension. I was frustrated, angry, resentful, wondering what I got ordained for. Since I could not get a transfer, I felt stuck.

Frank's situation was really much worse than mine. His pastor was 63 years old and weighed in at more than 300 pounds. The pastor's mother lived with them in the rectory. Mother and son did not like each other. The pastor spent most of his time and energy avoiding his mother. She was convinced that he was about to run off with a woman and leave her flat. Galloping paranoia! Frank was caught in the middle of this circus.

Frank and I spent an evening together at a reunion, and he told me all the stories of his rectory life. Instead of feeling frustration, he laughed. He saw only the humor. Before Frank was done with me, I was out of control laughing. The tears were rolling down my face. I returned to my own parish, and my pastor seemed downright dull.

You do always have a choice: anger or laughter.

WHAT DID WE TALK ABOUT before the O.J. Simpson affair? What was on the news? What did talk shows deal with? And the supermarket tabloids? I cannot remember. Can you?

If there is a lesson in all of this for us, it has to be that we should be careful about our heroes. We keep hoping (and expecting) that sports figures are going to be good examples for our children. We had better be realistic. How many disappointments do we need before we "get real?" Charles Barkley gave it to us straight. He said, "Just because I can play basketball, does not mean I should raise your kids." He was saying that he was too busy with himself to care about our kids. From what I can see, most sports figures feel this way. Charles is the only one honest enough to say it. Mr. Barkley is honest, but in my opinion, he is not a very nice man. But as he knows, he is not paid to be nice.

We all need heroes. Our children need role models. But we all need to be realistic. We are not likely to get them from the sports world, from the entertainment world, or from the political world. Jesus knew that money corrupts and power corrupts. If we traded places with some of the famous of our world, we might not do any better.

We still need role models. If Charles Barkley does not want the job, then we ordinary mortals must fill in. The father, the mother in every family is a more powerful role model than all of the Charles Barkleys of the world. Big sisters and big brothers are too, (not to mention parish priests.) If we all care enough to try, there will be worthy role models around.

I HAVE BEEN READING a book entitled "Black Holes and Time Warps" by Dr. Kip S. Thorns. It is a book about physics. It takes us from Newton through Einstein into the world of quantum physics. I understand only about half of this, and maybe 10% of the quantum physics part. That should be no great surprise. I cannot even figure out our rectory telephone system. The internal combustion engine is a total mystery to me. The world of physics could only be foreign territory for me.

When I finish this book, however, I suspect I will know a bit more. MIT will not be clamoring for my services, but the world of physics will be less mysterious. The more you know the less mystery there is. This system of learning seems to work in every field of study until you get to the mystery of God.

When we contemplate God, it strikes me that everything is in reverse. The more we learn about God, the less we understand. The more we deal with infinity, the greater the mystery becomes. Albert Einstein was the genius of the 20th Century. Physics was not a great mystery to him as it is to me. But with God it is different. I believe that no one experienced God more fully, more deeply than the 16th century Carmelite monk, St. John of the Cross. Yet, when he was through, I suspect that God was more of a mystery for him, than God is for you or me.

The idea seems to be that we do not get to the bottom of infinity. God is a mystery like no other created mystery. We will spend eternity exploring this mystery and we will never get to Graduation Day. The joy is in the exploring. That joy will never end. And it sure beats exploring quantum physics.

A S WE PREPARED TO BEGIN the school year, we formed a search committee to choose a new athletic director. A question was proposed during the interviews, "What would sportsmanship look like?" I thought that this was a great question. One can only do what one can imagine. What would sportsmanship look like? Teachers and coaches need to have some grasp of the answer.

I wanted to answer the question myself, but I was not being interviewed. I remember a high school basketball game in my Flint days, 38 years ago. The official in that game called a foul on a player. The young man thought it was a bad call. It may have been. I did not notice. The player jumped up and down for a minute and then sulked down the floor. The official walked beside him to the other end for the foul shot. The official kept looking at him, straight faces. The player would look back and then look away disgusted. Finally, the young man looked at the official and started to laugh. The official gave him a big smile and stuck out his hand, palm up. The player slapped it and went to his place. That is what sportsmanship looks like!

I thought about that exchange. I had been watching two classy individuals, one aged 40, the other 16. The older man provoked a response from the player by continuing to look at him. The younger man finally responded in a mature way. They were both wonderful. I did not know them. The whole exchange took about 8 seconds. And 38 years later, I can still remember the look on their faces. Classy is always memorable.

I LIVED IN ROME, ITALY for a period of four years. Of all the wonders of Rome, the least known are its fountains. Every piazza of any size has a fountain. St. Peter's Piazza has two. Most of the fountains of Rome are strikingly beautiful. The sculptor Gianlorenzo Bernini designed many of these fountains. Bernini was famous in Rome. He did so much to beautify the city.

Bernini came up from poverty and dreamed of fortune and fame. With his talents, all his dreams came true, and he hated it. It got so he could go nowhere without gathering a crowd. Later in life, he designed a sculpture piece, which stands in front of the church of Santa Maria sopra Minerva. It was a large elephant carrying a huge obelisk on its back. The elephant is Bernini and the obelisk is his fame. The message: Fame is a terrible burden to carry.

I get thinking about that burden as I see what is going on around all us. Our bishop is very sick and probably cannot come back to our diocese. Two men are working long hours to be elected President. Innumerable people are working hard to be elected to some public office. With the exception of the bishop, I do not necessarily like all these people. I might just have some question about their motivation. Yet, they do bear the burden of public life, the burden of fame. I certainly do not wish to bear that burden. I feel I owe such people a debt of gratitude.

We should watch our elected officials with a critical eye. That is the only way our country can work, but we need to remember the burdens that leaders carry. If we do not want to be the elephants upon which the obelisk is resting, we can at least thank God that there is someone so willing.

I N THE FOUR YEARS I studied in Rome, I took several trips
to Switzerland. My favorite spot was a little village named
Murren. Murren is on one side of a canyon. Across the
canyon is a whole range of mountain peaks, the most famous of
which is the JungFrau. To look out the window in Murren and see
the morning sun on all those peaks is beyond description. That
scene is breathtaking, the most beautiful sight in nature I have
ever seen. I often walked around the countryside or down in the
canyon with my mouth hanging open. Everywhere, there were lush
green hills and waterfalls. Yet I noticed the inhabitants would go
about their daily chores without seeming to notice.

I came to realize how much we are inclined to get used to
anything and take anything for granted. We can become seemingly
bored with even the most beautiful scenery in the world. We all
take the most precious gifts for granted. The people of Switzerland
are not the only ones so afflicted. We all have gifts that we never
think about. While living in Rome, I could look out my window
and see the dome of St. Peter's Basilica. It was so huge and seemed
close enough to reach out and touch a truly magnificent sight.
When I returned from Switzerland to Rome, I resolved that I would
spend a certain time each day just gaping at that dome.

Have you walked into the woods during the last few weeks? It is
spectacular. You will have so much to thank God for. The fall colors
of Michigan can put you in a completely different state of mind.
By the way, people of Switzerland do not take their country for
granted as one might think. They are grateful; they just do not act
like tourists.

I HAVE SPOKEN to a number of people lately who have voiced a feeling of unease. These are thoughtful people who do not have any particular reason for feeling uneasy. They feel as if they are not at home. This rings some bells inside of me because I often feel this way.

I recall years ago in a sociology class defining a marginal person as someone who did not fit in anywhere. The Italian immigrant was an example. This mythical Italian comes from Caserta near Naples in 1910. He settles in Providence, Rhode Island where he is a foreigner. He learns English, but never speaks it well. He works hard, is frugal, and gets rich by his standards. But he remains a foreigner. He dreams of Caserta, his home, where he strolled the streets in the cool of the evening. So finally, after 40 years, he returns to Caserta. His pocket is picked in the first half hour, and he finds that one must have a death wish to stroll the streets. It is then that he realizes that he does not really belong anywhere. He is living on the margins of two societies. He is a marginal person, not completely at home anywhere.

I think that we are all marginal people. We are not at home. Life is a temporary phenomenon, at least life here. Your feeling of belonging is an illusion. Life has a way of letting us know occasionally that we do not belong. I think that is the origin of a feeling of unease when everything seems to be going well.

God uses this feeling to remind us how much we need Him. God is saying, "Do not get too comfortable where you are because you must let go and move on." Marginal people can be very happy. They simply know what St. Augustine discovered in the 4th century, "Our hearts are restless until they rest in Thee."

So, welcome to marginal society. We are foreigners in a foreign land. We belong to God, and to nothing else.

W E USED TO PLAY a game in college. The game had no name. In it, I keep asking you the same question and you must give a different response. The question was simply, "Who are you?" At first, of course the answers are easy, just a matter of identity. But by the 20th question, it takes some thought. By the 30th, you are reaching into your soul for a response. The only problem with this game is that it can be too self-revealing.

It strikes me that this game could be a practice in spirituality throughout a lifetime. That question, "Who are you? Who am I?" is a very pertinent question regarding one's spirituality. "Who am I?" The answers should always be changing if I am growing. Because who I am is always changing. An even more pertinent question would be, "Who am I becoming?"

Our spiritual life is a journey toward God, or rather a journey into God. If we keep moving on the journey, naturally the scenery keeps changing. The question, "Who am I?" becomes "Where am I?" and, "Am I making progress in the journey into God?"

There are natural times of growth in a person's life. They are often painful times: times after the death of a loved one, times of sickness, times of renewal in life. During a time of great growth, I have seen people lose track of who they are. The journey is going so fast, they lose track. That is not bad, it is good. It is wonderful. Anyone getting closer to God is changing rapidly. The question, "Who am I?" becomes a very real question. Becoming is more real than being.

The question, "Who am I?" is a great question to carry through life.

L ONELINESS IS NOT a way of life; it is a part of life. Loneliness is a human experience we all have. It can be good, bad, a sickness or a gift. If loneliness is a way of life for a person, they need to think about how they could change their life and bring loved ones into it. Of course, some people have enforced loneliness, like prisoners in solitary confinement. They must find the strength within themselves to endure. No one envies them this task. But for almost all of us, loneliness is optional. We are stuck with some loneliness, but most of it we can do something about.

So what can we do? If you see loneliness as bad, you can try to escape from it. You can stay busy all the time. You can keep moving and be with people all the time. In this, you will probably fail. You will get very tired, and you will discover that you can be most lonely in a crowd of people. Loneliness need not be a way of life, as if it is all you have. Usually, people can change such engulfing loneliness. But loneliness is a part of life. You cannot escape it completely.

And you should not! Because loneliness is not bad, it is a gift from God. Our loneliness forces us to draw inside and find ways to be happy alone. Loneliness forces us to find ways to love ourselves and to enjoy our own company. If you do not know how to be alone and enjoy it, you may not be fit for the company of others.

See loneliness as a gift. No one ever achieved depth of character without learning how to live fruitfully with their loneliness. I hope we can all have a balance in our lives, enough loneliness and enough intimacy. Both are precious gifts.

I T IS EASIER TO REACT than to think. In my history, I have been the owner of two bulldogs. I watched them waddle their way through life. I learned a lot about dogs, and much about myself. All that these two creatures did was react. They reacted to food, to the opposite gender, to other dogs intruding. Their reactions were completely predictable. And I learned that I, all too often, was walking through life reacting. The human race is about five million years from bulldogs. Yet, it seemed that I had not climbed very far up the evolutionary tree.

We human beings have the capacity to think in every situation. We also have the ability to react. We can choose the second course, but only if we want to live like a bulldog. When anything happens, we can respond in any number of ways. We can react based on our emotions in a predictable way. Or we can think and respond in any number of ways.

If someone insults me, I can respond by thinking. I do not need to react in anger. I can think about ways to respond. I can imagine the best way to handle the situation. I can imagine the most mature and generous way to respond. And if I can imagine a person acting in that way, I can do it. I have the capacity to always choose the best, most mature way to treat another person. Human beings always have an option to choose the best.

The freedom to choose, this is what puts us above animals. We can choose; they can only react. It is easier to react. St. Bernard said, "The human person fully alive is the Glory of God." We have no business living like bulldogs.

PEOPLE OFTEN GIVE UP just when they are about to achieve success. This saying is all too true in my experience. We work for a goal; we work and work and we get tired. We can easily become discouraged and quit just before it all falls together. Sometimes, we can work so hard but we must wait for God to work on the problem. We can quit too soon.

I have seen people quit on their marriage when, I thought, they were on the verge of real break through. Then they find some one else and do all the same work to achieve a superior marriage. All of this calls for the wisdom on our part to see when our goal is hopeless and when it is really possible. There is no virtue working on a dead horse. We need wisdom not to quit too soon.

Our bishop in Saginaw has said, "The difference between greatness and mediocrity may be two inches." That is my recurring nightmare. Someday I will be with God and He will say, "Jimmy, you were two steps away from greatness. Why didn't you take them?" I will not be condemned by the lack of those two steps. I will be embarrassed by my failure to take them.

Let us wake up and have the wisdom to see where we are. We do not want to quit when success is right on top of us. For any one of us, greatness may be just two steps away.

"THE AWARENESS of ambiguity of one's highest achievements (and failures) is a definite sign of maturity." - Paul Tillich, philosopher/theologian

One of the Beatitudes says, "Blessed are the single hearted." This means blessed are those who act for one motive alone. I am afraid there are not many so blessed. As human beings, we usually have multiple motives for each act. Some motives are virtuous and honorable and some are considerably less than honorable. We tend to acknowledge the virtuous motives and not see the selfish ones. The eminent Lutheran theologian urges us to see our ambiguity.

Our ego is usually the villain. For example, a young man gets accepted to Harvard Medical School. He says he is doing this to better serve people. True! But he is also doing it to please his parents, to impress his girlfriend, to enable him to strut around the neighborhood. Finally, he gets even with Sister Mary Whoever, who called him a dummy during 3rd grade. All these things motivate him. It is important that he knows his motives and recognizes which predominates. That is maturity.

T.S. Eliot's play about St. Thomas Becket has him resisting a temptation by saying, "This last temptation was the greatest treason; to do the right thing for the wrong reason." We must know what we are about.

A good sign of false motivation is when I begin to enjoy myself too much. And so, I must correct my brother priest's mistakes. It is my duty. But if I am giggling while I do it, I had better question my motives. It is such fun to work on the faults of others.

I must remember that I am not single-hearted. The last single-hearted act was when God said, "Let there be light." Since that time, all acts have multiple motivations. We are ambiguous people. We must learn to recognize and live with our ambiguity. It is the beginning of maturity.

HOW COME ANGELS can fly? Because they hold themselves lightly. If we take ourselves too seriously, we have so much to defend. A large ego can keep us busy all the time. We can be like a dog defending his territory. The bigger the territory he stakes out for himself, the busier he is. We cannot afford all that ego. There are too many other things to do in life. We cannot afford to be defending territory.

The healthiest thing that we can do is to learn to laugh at ourselves. Laughter will destroy ego quicker than anything else. If we can only imagine God reacting to His children, He must laugh a lot. We are so self-important. Remember the question, "How can we make God laugh?" By telling Him what we are going to do tomorrow.

As we go through life, we can laugh with God. We often take ourselves so seriously. If we step outside ourselves for a moment, we can see how ridiculous it all is. And we can laugh with God. The trick is to see ourselves as God sees us. Then all the pretence can drop away.

Then we can laugh.

I N PRAYER, what we usually ask of God is that two and two not make four. The type of prayer referred to above is what I call "Fire House" spirituality. When we are in desperate shape, we put an emergency call to God saying, "Put the fire out." In the call, we usually forget to mention that we ourselves started the fire.

Fire House prayers are recited by drunks after a night of drinking when they drive home. The prayer goes, "If you keep the cops off me, I will never drink again." Of course, I have no personal acquaintance with this type of prayer.

This kind of prayer is asking that two and two not make four. We pray that God will not allow the natural consequences of our actions to happen. We say "God, save me from myself." God does seem to answer such prayers, or else we just get lucky. If we were God, we would never answer such prayers.

If we have developed a longing for self-defeating behavior, prayer is not the solution. Changing our behavior is. I know people who figuratively shoot themselves in the foot every morning and then pray God will take away the pain. Fire House spirituality!

In real spirituality, we must start by praying for willingness. We must be willing to want what God wants. Then our prayers will be answered. We can find ourselves praying that God will give us what we do not want. He will not do that. Example: I want to get home without the cops, but I do not want a sober life. Example: I want my child to get good marks in school, but I do not want to take the trouble to supervise. I want my kids to change, but I do not want to.

Speaking of school, two and two will always make four. And God will not consistently respond to "Fire House" prayers.

I F YOU WERE RAISED in the home of Genevieve O'Leary, my mother, you learned the poem, "Elegy Written in a Country Church-Yard" by Thomas Gray at an early age. One of the best verses in Gray's Elegy states:

> "Full many a flower is born to blush unseen,
> And waste its sweetness on the desert air."

It is a beautiful line. My question is, is it true? Are beautiful people born to be wasted? Does greatness in people sometimes blush unseen? We all know about greatness. Is there greatness we do not know about? Is there a Mozart out there whose mom and dad never got him piano lessons? Is there a Picasso who was too poor to do anything but survive?

I am convinced that such people exist. Vincent Van Gogh made about 50 bucks in his whole life as a painter. Now, his paintings go for millions. Henry David Thoreau wrote "Walden." When he died, they found 167 copies of the three hundred published in the back room of his house. A hundred years later, "Walden" is still in print! It is a classic! But in his day, Henry David's wisdom was rather unnoticed. He did a lot of "blushing unseen."

Do saints go unnoticed? Can personal greatness attract no attention? Of course, it can! Most saints are not canonized. Had St. Therese of Lisieux not been a Carmelite, no one would have ever heard of her. There is greatness around us if we look for it. I see people who are incredibly loving under much stress. I see people who seem to be able to bear any burden with patience, even with joy. They will never be famous.

However, they may "blush unseen," but they do not "waste their sweetness." People who become great people affect those around them. They do not change the world. They change their part of it. And for them, it is enough.

NOVEMBER IS THE TIME we think about the deceased. It need not be morbid. We can remember our deceased with joy, with gratitude, and certainly with love. We can even think about death in a positive way. Death, the event, is okay, but the process stinks. The event is the going to God. That is glorious. The process is more troublesome. No one dies of good health. The process is painful and tedious. We are not supposed to like it. But we get beyond the process. Thank God. Medicine has progressed to the point where the worst of the pain can be eliminated.

Many of us have watched people die. As a priest and a hospice volunteer for six years, I have seen many die. For me, the occasion is always filled with awe. I have seen people do it well, and not so well. I have seen people die with total awareness and acceptance of what was going on. I have seen people die denying the whole process to their last breath. All this experience makes me think of how I would like to die. We only get one chance to die. I would like to do it well. I have a feeling that if I am able to accept all reality from God graciously, I will be able to accept the reality of death graciously.

I would like the circumstance of my death to be quiet and peaceful. However, I cannot control that. This is up to God. We can only hope and pray. I recall wonderful deaths, one of them my father's. The dying persons were surrounded by loved ones and the pain was bearable or absent. They were aware and knew what was going on. You cannot do better than that. That is how I would like death to come to me.

How about you? What is the last thing you desire to see before you close your eyes in death? A healthy November thought!

I WAS VISITING some friends at their cottage in Northern Michigan a few years ago. There were four of us together for a few days over a weekend: myself, the father of the family, the mother, and a 17-year-old daughter. On Saturday, I asked my friend Jack how he wanted to handle Mass. He said they usually went on Sunday morning at the local church. I offered to celebrate Mass at his home for the four of us and any neighbors who might wish to come. Jack thought that was a great idea. So, we planned for Mass late Sunday afternoon.

Sunday morning mother and daughter had a big fight. It was about some minor matter. They did some yelling and then sunk into cold silence. Jack was caught in the middle, as usual, and he was in very bad humor. By late afternoon, no one was speaking to anyone, and we were about to celebrate the Lord's Supper! No one else came, so it was just the four of us hostile people. I was thinking, "Why didn't I attend Mass at church this morning?"

I had to get it over with. The four of us sat at a card table. I read the readings, gave no homily, and tried to get through the Mass as quickly as possible. I felt that this just might be the worst celebration of Mass I had ever had. But I was not watching; something was happening.

I finished Mass with relief. But no one moved; no one spoke. It seemed like an hour. Finally, mother said, "I wouldn't yell at you if I didn't love you." With that, the tears began. And then the hugs. The Mass can bring out the best in any of us. The Lord's Supper brought us all together, as it was meant to do.

I had thought this to be the worst Mass I had celebrated. But, I was not watching. It turned out to be one of the best.

I RECENTLY HAD AN encounter with a woman at a meeting. I found her quite striking. She was a daughter and a mother, and caught in the squeeze. She told us that for years her mother had been very troubled by alcoholism. The whole family had suffered. As the eldest daughter, she especially suffered in this dysfunctional family. She held resentment against her mother who now lived next door and for whom she was the principal caregiver. She said she would like to tell her mother the truth about her feelings but she felt that her mother was just too old and too sick to comprehend such a confrontation. She would be dumping on an old woman, and she said she would not do that.

At the same time, this woman had an appointment the next day in an alcoholic treatment center. Her daughter was recuperating there and had asked her to come to "Family Day." On such a day, her daughter could and would point out to her how she had failed as a mother. At least this is what she anticipated would happen. She understood that her daughter would need to do this for her own recovery.

As a good daughter, she could not "dump" on her own mother. As a good mother, she had to allow her daughter to "dump" on her. She said, "I was born in the wrong generation." To my amazement, this woman could laugh at this completely absurd and unfair situation. I suspect that her mother will never know what a loving daughter she had. I do hope her daughter might some day know what a loving mother she had. That is the truth of the matter.

"BE CAREFUL what you pray for. You might get it." This slogan simply implies that we do not know what it will take to make us happy. We think we know. Experience shows us that we do not. For 10 years, I prayed that a certain situation would develop. It finally did and I thanked God. That very situation soon became the vertical bar on my cross. Be careful what you pray for.

In Coldwater, I celebrated Mass every week in the Lakeland Prison for men. Of course, everyone there dreamed of the day they would get out. They were all convinced that all they needed to be happy was to get out. I would ask them to look beyond that fence and see the people walking around. Were they all happy? We all need more for happiness than just a lack of confinement. Mine was not a message men in prison were inclined to accept.

What do you need in the next five years to make you happy? Maybe you think you know. I am sure that I do not know. The longer I live, the more I leave that question in the hands of God. (Priests, by the way, seldom ask for a particular assignment. That way, if they do not like their parish, they can always blame the bishop.) I would rather leave my future in God's hands.

I would hazard a guess about our future. Whatever we will need to be happy, I would guess that it is something "inside" of us and not "outside." Happiness has to do with attitude, not job, or sessions. Attitude is an "inside" affair.

A WISE MAN ONCE SAID, "The most important thing we do in life is 'show up.'"

What he is telling us is that the purpose of life is to live, to live in a proper way. For a Christian, this means to live in a loving way, loving toward God, loving toward others.

In our society, we can become so goal-oriented that we forget about living. I have known men who worked like beavers for their children. They wanted to leave their wives and children well off, but they worked so hard and long that they never really got to know their children. They worked so hard they forgot to live.

As a parish priest, I can arrive at a parish with all sorts of ideas as to what I should accomplish in that parish. Priests commonly talk about "bringing the parish along" to some desired point. And that, I think, is missing the mark. A priest comes to a parish to live, to share life. Sharing spirituality is the same as sharing life. I was in my last parish for 10 years. That was a blessing. I finally got the message that I was there to live, not to achieve some short-term goal.

To share life with others is a full agenda for any of us. To share our experience, strength and hope, to share fears and dreams, to share our love for God and for each other: this is a full plate. Life is so rich. All we need to do is live each moment fully. Living fully the life God gives us today is the most important thing we do. Life is there. We need to "show up."

Fine words.

I NEED TO TALK about Honduras. The trouble is that my thoughts about my experience there are all a jumble. It will take me time to sort out all these thoughts. Someone asked me, "What did you find surprising in Honduras?"

I was surprised to experience how poverty is a state of mind. It is not just deprivation of material things. Poor people, really poor people, are very limited in their thinking. Most people only get a few years of schooling. If they go to the 6th grade, families cannot see what use it is to send their children any longer. They just assume that everything will remain the same. A farmer's son will be a farmer. There is no other possibility. Poverty tends to be a state of mind. Before people can move beyond poverty, they need to approach their problems differently. That is what Fr. Cook is trying to teach his children at Mission Honduras. Schooling develops different states of mind.

I was also surprised at how happy and charming the people were in Honduras. I think of poverty as grinding people down until they are listless or bitter or both. To me, that did not appear to be happening in people. The children, adults and the elderly, were charming and always grateful for whatever we did. One 70-year-old woman wanted to give a blessing to one of our doctors in gratitude. When told that would be all right, she put her hand over his heart and prayed that God would always be there. Not a dry eye in the room! We encountered gracious people.

EVERYONE WANTS to live well off. Many would say they want to live rich. I am of the latter group. However, there are all sorts of ways of defining what living rich means.

To the secular world, living rich means that you have the money to buy what you want. If you are really living rich, you have enough to buy whatever you want. Christ, of course, would have a different definition of living rich. I think that Christ would look at relationships, not money, to judge the richness of life. I think Christ would say that if you are surrounded with loved ones and friends, you are rich. And if the friendships run deep, you are very rich. I like those standards.

In my family, we had the expression, "Some one has done well!" That meant they were successful in business. They made a lot of money. I always bristled when I heard this expression. I always wanted to point to a carpenter who was laid off for the winter and used the extra time to deepen his relationship with his children. I would say that he has done well.

We live rich by the depth of our friendships, not by the quantity of our bank accounts.

I HAVE FOUND MUCH to admire in some of the religious practices of our Native American Indians. The Navahos have a custom that astonishes me. They weave these large blankets, and I am told that in the large ones, which have a border, they always weave in a flaw, purposely. The line with the flaw is called the "spirit line." The flaw is always in the lower left hand corner. Its purpose is to remind the weaver that perfection is not absence of FLAW. The Navaho idea of perfection is the ability of the whole to lift up the defect to its own level of perfection.

I find this to be an incredible thought. A very healthy thought. It means that perfection does not demand a perfect record. It means that we can embrace our faults. It means that it is never too late to be perfect. It means that we can be redeemed. With the grace of God, we can transform our life and lift it up. The whole of ourselves can lift the worst of ourselves to a higher lever.

In living, we are not playing a symphony. A few sour notes in the first movement do not ruin the whole piece. Perfection is compatible with some wrong moves. We can relax and keep working.

The Navahos can teach us a thing or two. Perfection is not the absence of flaw. Perfection is the ability of the whole to lift the flaw to its own level. This is so healthy. We do not get neurotic on this idea. We get relaxed.

P AIN IS SOMETHING that we would all like to avoid if possible. I love my dentist, but I do not love walking into his/her office. In the garden, Jesus showed that He did not like pain any better than the rest of us. Yet, pain is a natural part of life. We pretend that pain is an abnormality. When in pain, we react! Something is wrong. Who is to blame? What can I do about this? What can I take to feel better? This last question is a splendid background for alcohol-drug addictions.

Actually, pain is most frequently a call from God. God calls us to change by way of pain. In all honesty, we would not be inclined to listen to any other kind of call. When I feel on top of life, why would I want to change anything? When pain comes along, I listen; I respond; I obey. If God wants to get my attention, He should not send an angel; a toothache would do the trick much better.

I think we must always take a careful look at pain in our lives. Pain might be an evil person affecting us. Or pain most probably is God trying to get His message across. His message is that it is time to change, time to grow up. God is currently getting the message to me, "Grow up!" The world does not need another 60-year-old adolescent. God does tend to be blunt!

When pain comes, we should listen. God knows, better than we do how to make us happy. Led by God, we will get beyond pain.

A FEW YEARS AGO, I spent some time with one of my favorite groups of friends. They are a heavy-duty crowd and we were talking about some serious topics. One member of the crowd proposed a question: "What do you really want in life? What are you looking for?" Another very thoughtful person in the group answered immediately, "Intimacy" he said. "I want intimacy in life. Intimacy with men, with women, with children and most of all with God."

That response got all of us talking—and thinking. The more I thought, the more I recognized this as a great response. Intimacy is truly the richest of human experiences. Real intimacy is the deepest sharing of our innermost selves with another person; the deepest sharing of which we are capable. We are most fully human when we are able to give ourselves to another so completely. We can be very willing to serve other people but very unwilling to give of ourselves in a personal way. To attempt intimacy is always to take a risk. Intimacy is a scary experience.

My friend who sought intimacy was of course, not thinking of sexuality. He was thinking of friendship, the deepest kind of friendship. We use the word "friend" so often and in so many ways that it loses its true flavor. The word "friend" is one of the richest words in our language. To be a friend in the fullest sense is impossible. In this life, we cannot give ourselves that fully to another. But we keep trying, and that is how we become fully human. The experience of intimate friendship adds more spice to our life than anything else does. Mixing with people is "where it's at."

In eternity, God will teach us all intimacy. Until then, intimacy with God is open to us, based on our faith. That is the process of prayer. Reaching for intimacy with God adds spice to our life too. That kind of reaching will go on for all eternity.

So, what do you want out of life? Think about intimacy.

W E MEET GOD IN SILENCE. Is there another way? When I was very young, growing up in Lansing, an old man in our neighborhood went to a movie every day. Since I had only seen a movie a few times in my life, I thought that this was an incredible luxury. Now, 60 years later, anyone with a TV set could see 8 or 10 movies each day, enough to turn the brain to mush. The richest kings of the Middle Ages could not afford one hundredth of the entertainment we take for granted.

In the past, a huge amount of boredom was presumed in every life. Most ordinary people did not travel more than 5 miles from the house where they were born. That boredom made people religious. Going to church and listening to a long sermon was the best excitement in the village. In a more positive way, boredom left time for God. People were not too busy to spend time with God. More important, boredom created silence for God. The world of the Middle Ages was a much quieter place than today. Silence leaves room for God. I do not say people found God then any better than now, but they had some natural advantages.

I once visited a deserted 19th century mining village. It seemed like boredom was a built in part of life there too. The records showed that one winter they brought in 10 wagon loads of food and 20 wagon loads of whiskey. They handled boredom. They got stoned!

We have endless entertainment. We manage to escape boredom in a myriad of ways. We escape silence in the same way. And there lies our danger. When we cannot tolerate silence in our lives, we avoid any very deep encounters with God. In every spiritual tradition in the world, silence is a treasure and a necessity for growth. We consider silence a drag.

God lives in silence, and that is where we must find Him. If we want a close relationship with God, if we want intimacy, there is no other way. We need to spend quiet time with God every day, every single day. We cannot let our entertainment capabilities overwhelm us.

GARRISON KEILLOR named his fictional Catholic church in his hometown of Lake Wobegon, "Our Lady of Perpetual Responsibility." He was being nice. He really meant, "Our Lady of Perpetual Guilt."

Older generations of Catholics feel that the Catholic church heaped a lot of guilt upon them in their earlier years. There were so many "shoulds" and, when we fell short as was inevitable, we got lots of guilt. This was not true of my home parish in Lansing, but I am sure that it was true of many places.

Let us talk about guilt and shame. I believe that the real problem is not with guilt, but with shame. According to my definition, guilt is my bad feeling about what I have done. Shame is my bad feeling about me. When we become aware that our actions hurt others, we should feel guilty. That is the result of a good conscience in action.

Shame is another emotion entirely. Shame is our bad feeling about who we are. It is very destructive. We are more than our actions. Our actions reveal us. They reveal that we are maybe careless, maybe insensitive, maybe stupid, maybe all of the above. Our bad actions do not reveal that we are bad. God can make the distinction; He knows our hearts.

Shame comes from a lack of love. We feel bad about ourselves because we were not loved when we should have been. Many feel shame. They do not feel lovable because they were not loved. Shame is a mistake. God loves us all, and He is the most important person in our lives.

We need to feel guilt at times. We do bad things. No one needs shame. No one deserves shame. We are children of God, loved by Him. Reserve our bad feelings for our actions, not for ourselves. We do not belong to a church named "Our Lady of Perpetual Shame." Thank God.

I NSIDE AND OUTSIDE feminist circles, God is now often referred to as "She." This is sometimes spoken in a laughing manner, but often seriously. So, what is the scoop? Is God male or female?

I do not believe I can give the definite word on this question. I am not the Pope. Actually, I do not think he can either. In God, we find the Ultimate Mystery, the Infinite Mystery. Of course, "He/She" is neither male nor female. He is Mystery. Nothing we say about God is totally or really true. God is so far beyond our experience that we have no words to use for Him. We cannot call God "It" so we are left with "He" or "She." Neither word reflects the proper reality, but they are all we have. Since our religion developed in a patriarchal society, we naturally used the male word for God. To do anything else would have made this religion incomprehensible to its people. However, it could have been otherwise.

In the past, at workshops and classes, which I have led, I have asked the participants for one-word expressions of God, as they know God. I always get a stream of words like: loving, caring, nurturing, guiding, teaching, hugging, and nursing. To me these words have a female bend. Truly, males can teach, nurture and hug. However, when you think about these experiences, I will bet you think female. Although we say "He" for God, it seems that we are thinking "She."

I do believe I will go on calling God "He." To say God-He/She is simply too awkward. However, I am aware that as I say "He," I am thinking "She." I must admit that the female image rings truer than the male to me. I am also aware that God is shrouded in mystery. Neither word really fits.

L ET US GET POETIC AGAIN. T. S. Eliot wrote of our human journey in the following words:

> We shall not cease from exploration
> And the end of all our exploring
> Will be to arrive where we started
> And know the place for the first time.

These words have long been favorites of mine. They are profound. They were written by a man who knew what the human journey was all about.

In the beginning of our lives, we tried to discover what kind of people we were. We all too soon were sidetracked onto what kind of things we liked. We explored and explored. We wanted to be happy, and the source of that happiness was all laid out there in the world. The material things of our world would make us happy. This is a phase. We can pass through it. Some people never do so. They grasp at "things" endlessly to be happy, and never make it.

Others learn that in "things" is not where happiness is. They learn that instead of reaching outward, they must turn inward for happiness. Then the fruitful exploration begins. Inside we find our true self, not the self that TV ads tell us we are. We are not consuming machines. We are images of God bound for eternity. Inside we find God, and we can explore how He touches us, how He leads us, how He loves us. This is a lifelong exploration, and that gives us joy.

With this exploration of our insides, we find ourselves back where we started — discovering what kind of people we are. The end of our exploring is to know who we really are. God leads us to this place and gives us the gift; the wisdom to see it for the first time. "That place, where we begin, where we end is our own heart."

A FEW YEARS AGO, I heard a radio talk show. The host was talking on the subject of prayer and cloistered nuns who were dedicated to prayer. The host could only think of one reason to pray: to beg God to change His mind when He was about to send evil on the world. He thought that for people who frequently prayed, "Thy will be done," this was a contradictory exercise! In one breath we say, "Thy will be done," and in the next breath we say, "Please don't do this. Change your mind."

The radio commentator was using deadly logic. I cannot fault that. But his starting point was wrong. To presume that the only reason we pray is to get God to change His mind is nonsense. The lives of cloistered nuns are not spent coaxing God to send "goodies" to us instead of pain. The nuns are not professional beggars. The primary reason for prayer is to commune with God. Just to be consciously with God is the reason for prayer. When we spend time with God, we fulfill and enrich ourselves. We become who we really are and who God wants us to be. We are not asking God to change His mind. We are becoming what He wants us to be.

The radio host has a cheap idea of prayer, and a cheap attitude. It strikes me that we Catholics talk about prayer in such a way as though we are trying to get something God really does not want to give us. This gives a wrong impression about prayer. We speak of prayers that "really work." It sounds so utilitarian, like magic.

Prayer is simply spending time with God. What cloistered nuns do is spend a lifetime with God. Of course, we can ask God for favors. But if that is all prayer is for us, there is something wrong. My suggestion: we pray only for knowledge of God's will and the power to carry that out. We never ask God to change His mind. We do not have to. God only wants what is best for us.

I F YOUR GOD comes to your rescue and gets you out of
trouble, it is time you started looking for the true God. The
search for God is a constant calling in our life. As soon as we
think we have God figured out, then we need to start all over
again. God is infinite. To get to the bottom of God is indeed an
infinite journey. With God, all we can do is search. We never get
to the end.

I hear people talk about God as a problem solver. Sometimes
God is just that for us. But not always! Perhaps a thousand babies
died in the northern part of Africa last month. God loved every
one of them, and yet He did nothing. Why? I do not know. I would
not presume to explain infinity. God is more than a problem solver;
and sometimes He is less than a problem solver. If you have
decided that God is, or should be, one who pulls your nickels out of
the fire, then it is time to start looking again for the real God. The
search must go on.

We cannot get to the end of our search, even in eternity. No
image of God is adequate. Some are better than others, but none
fills the bill. The search goes on forever. That is Good News. Each
day we have the joy of discovering a "New God." That joy never
ends, unless we are stuck on today's image or yesterday's image.

So, I say to you, "Suspect the image you have formed of God. It
will please Him more than adoration."

W E ARE NEARING the end of the church year. The readings remind us of our final judgment. It might be a good time to get reflective about our past. I pose this question: "What is the one experience which alone would justify your life?" Take your time. You have from now 'til the end of the world to find an answer! Wow!

Let your memory go wild. When were you at your best in life? What have you done in your past that you are most proud of? What one act would you like to repeat? For all of us, when did we reach our peak? I would hazard a guess that we may have hit our best moment when we were young. It seems to me that I was a lot more generous way back when. Maybe that is just wishful fantasy.

In God's eyes, our moment could well have been some minor incident in our lives. Our best act may have been a decision inside us that no one would know about except God. It is possible that your most heroic act could have been to keep your mouth closed in a time of stress.

So, when was your high point? What action in the past would alone justify your life? If it has not happened yet, it had better happen soon. You do want to miss your finest hour.

ALL PEOPLE CARRY within them thoughts that have the power to bring them instant peace. A few years ago, a movie was produced about God returning to the human race. I think it was just called "God," but I cannot remember. This time God did not come in the form of a baby in a manger, but in the form of an old man, George Burns, to be exact. (Who else?). God, George Burns style, was kind, gentle, patient, wise and of course, wonderfully funny. With almighty power, one can pull some marvelous jokes on people.

God returned to give His people a message. That message was simple: "You have all that you need to make it work." A wondrous message! God says, "You have all you need; use it." The whole movie was rather silly but the message was profound. Christ and His message did it all for us. Christ did not take all struggles out of life. He did not intend to. But He gave us what we need to develop ourselves into what God wants us to be. He gave us enough to continue His creation of this world.

In light of Hollywood's version of God's message, people today are so filled with worry and anxiety, with anger and fear. Yet, we carry the solution within us. We cannot completely control our thoughts. However, we do have some control. We can think right thoughts that will bring peace. We have the power. Circumstances do not bring us peace of mind. We have the God-given power within to do that job.

All people carry within them thoughts that have the power to bring them peace.

SOONER OR LATER, most of us discover a basic fact about life. It can be boring. No matter what your life or your job is like, life eventually boils down to a certain sameness. That does not mean that what you are doing in life is not important. You may be doing a very important job, but it can still be boring. Raising children is very important, but it is not always exciting. (Then again, at times, it may be too exciting.)

I think that boredom is a simple fact of life. It happens. It is just a matter of time. There is so much excitement in falling in love. But, before long, something happens. That face that you felt you could never tire of looking at, you get tired of looking at. It is more exciting to fall in love than to be in love. Loving means "being there" for the loved one, and that is not always exciting.

I think that boredom is a spiritual problem. We do not suffer from boredom because of what is happening on our outside, but because of the condition of our insides. If our prayer makes us aware of all that is going on around us, we will not feel that we are "spinning our wheels."

When anyone reflects on their life, and hears themselves ask, "Is this all there is?" all the spiritual alarms should go off. It is not time to change your life; it is time to change your viewpoint. It is time to see the world around you in a different way.

Boredom is a force in life. It can be good or bad. Boredom can be a wake-up call to draw inside and get closer to God. Boredom can help us get God's viewpoint in our lives.

WHERE DO WE FIND our joy in life? This is a very fundamental spiritual question. The answer shows us where we are. It is so easy to say we are in God's world and then find all our joy in material things. The question makes us ask, "Who is kidding whom?" If all my joy comes from things, I am not a spiritual person.

I was raised with the idea that all saints were horrible ascetics who took no pleasure in any created things. This is all nonsense. Saints took great pleasure wherever pleasure was to be found, but they also found pleasure in God and spirituality. Look at St. Francis who gloried in the beauty of nature. However, material pleasure can lead us astray. If they are the only pleasures we find in life, then we are not living in God's world. Way back in the Book of Wisdom, the author advised his readers, "Let the beauty of nature lead you to the beauty of the Creator."

We cannot help but enjoy the pleasures of the world. I think that Jesus expected His followers to discover during their lives that there are more important pleasures than just the material kind. He expected His followers to develop a taste for those kinds of pleasures. As they grew older, that taste would grow. When we are old and sick and the material pleasures wilt away, the higher pleasures will still bring us joy.

Where do you find your joy? It is a crucial question. Is it time to look inside?

ENCOURAGEMENT FROM A TEACHER can turn a student's life around. When I read the above sentence, it reminds me of a little boy we shall call Vince. He was an orphan; he had no direction in his life. He attended a Catholic school. At the time of our story, he was in the fourth grade. He was quickly becoming a very disruptive influence in the school. He was a "bad kid." The pastor of the parish did not approve of him and did not like him. The pastor wanted Vince out of his school.

Vince's teacher was a middle-aged nun. She was very tough. She did not like girls. She did not like good boys either. She liked bad boys. She liked Vince, which meant that she was "on him" like a bee on a bulldog. Whenever he did something wrong, which was most of the time, he faced Sister. She was tough. She looked more like a Green Bay Packer linebacker than a sweet nun.

One day in 1905, the pastor stormed into Sister's classroom. "Vincent, stand up," he shouted. Vince did. "Vincent, sit down," Sister said. Then she backed the priest out of the classroom door. In the hall, she said, "Two rules: You never barge into my classroom in that rude way. If you have a problem with Vincent, you come to me." End of discussion.

Historical note: In 1905, nuns did not speak to priests in this fashion, with, of course, one exception.

I suspect Sister knew what she was doing. She saved a life at that moment. Vince worshiped her. Her word was law from then on. And she made his life miserable. She demanded responsibility from him. She demanded and demanded. She saved a life.

She did me a favor too. Vince was my father.

ONCE IN A WHILE, you know someone about whom you say, "Thank God I know him." Just knowing some people is enriching, and you must be grateful. There is a man who lives in Bronson, Michigan who is such a person for me. He is such a person for many people. I will call him Frankie.

Frankie lives in a custodial care home for the disabled. Frankie has always lived with Cerebral Palsy; at least I think that is his disease. He is unable to walk and has very little arm and hand control. Frankie can only speak with great difficulty. Even with all of his problems of communication, Frankie has as many good friends as the average professional man I know.

His secret seems to be that Frankie is such a happy, beautiful person, that people find him unforgettable. Everyone around Frankie learns to love him very quickly. He is patient and uncomplaining. I have always found Frankie to be fun, humorous and full of joy. He is living proof that one does not have to talk to communicate love.

In our society, Frankie is not considered "normal." He has never learned to be competitive. He has never "beat" anyone at anything. He has always had to accept help with even the simplest tasks of life. All he has ever learned from this experience is gratitude. Frankie never learned to try to "win." He only learned to try to live. He never won a race. He never shot a bird. He never won an argument. He never did so many things that make the rest of us so gloriously "normal."

I never considered Frankie normal. I only thought him wonderful. Frankie is now sick and close to death. I thank God I know him.

"IT WAS THE BEST OF TIMES. It was the worst of times." So begins "The Tale of Two Cities," Dickens great novel about the French Revolution. It is a great beginning. It makes me think. If this were the best of times, would I know it? Would you?

We are in the midst of the wonderful holidays of the year. Thanksgiving and Christmas are, to me, the most family-oriented holidays. And I think families have a "golden age," a time when everyone is at the right age to appreciate the holidays and enjoy each other. The younger kids are old enough to really enter into the family discourse and the older kids are still young enough to be filled with wonder at this beautiful season of the year.

I remember Thanksgiving days when my siblings and parents seemed at the perfect time of life to enjoy each other. I can remember walking to Midnight Mass through the snow with my family and feeling that everything was just as it should be. "God's in His heaven; all's right with the world."

I ask you, is your family at such a "golden age?" I hope it is. Most of all, if this is the "best of times," I hope you are aware of that wonderful fact. I do not think that I ever was aware when Christmas for me was at its best.

Whether this is the best or the worst of times, Thanksgiving and Christmas are still magic. May you enjoy this gift of God.

WHAT WOULD your world be like if you were always at your best? I think we could safely say that, your loved ones would be happier. Suppose you could take a pill every morning and for that day, you would be at your best. Wonderful! Of course, there is no such pill, but if there was, it would be called the "Gratitude Pill."

I think that a spirit of Thanksgiving does just that to anyone; it brings out the very best inside us. One cannot imagine a truly grateful person being mean-spirited. Gratitude lifts us up above all the problems of daily life. Gratitude breeds generosity. And more important for each of us, gratitude breeds happiness. Most of us have so many blessings. If we are thinking of what we have in gratitude, we are bound to be happy.

Gratitude is not a casual element in Christianity. It is basic. Christ tells us that God first loved us. Before we did anything, before we became worthy of anything, God first loved us. Our only response can be gratitude, or perhaps awe and gratitude. Gratitude is so basic that Christians named what we now call the Mass the "Eucharistia," the Thanksgiving. The Mass is our basic way of experiencing and celebrating our faith. We express and celebrate by saying "Thank you." Whenever we celebrate Mass together, we need to ask, "What are we grateful for?" Every Mass is a reminder to call up gratitude in our minds. Every Mass is a call to be emotionally healthy, to be happy.

Gratitude is to be a way of life, not an occasional emotion. We do not need to wait for Thanksgiving. We can feel gratitude anytime we choose to keep our minds on the right things. If we look at our gifts, we will be grateful. And we can do that every day. Gratitude just might be our best means to personal happiness. It also just might be the most neglected means. I hope not for me. I hope not for you.

H OW GRATEFUL would you be to anyone who did for you what you have done for God?

We rightfully try to concentrate on all that God has done for us. This way of thinking does and should lead us to gratitude. But it can be a healthy exercise to turn this thinking around. Guilt and shame consume so many people. We can serve God faithfully and then do one bad thing, and we think God will only concentrate on our sin. A loving God would have better vision than that. We can think of what we have done for God. We know we are sinners, but that is not the whole picture. We call an examination of conscience taking a moral inventory. Yet, we only look at sin. It really is taking an "immoral" inventory. We should look at both sides.

We see what people do for God and what we do for God. I see Mothers and Fathers willing to give anything for their children. I see teachers giving of themselves for the good of children. I see people being loyal to friends under extreme stress. I see priests embracing a way of life as unnatural as celibacy for the sake of God's people. If anyone did these things for me, I would be astonished. I would be grateful beyond measure.

God is infinitely better than any one of us. If we should be grateful, think of God's gratitude. God has complete vision. He sees more than sin. We should not be so afraid of complacency that we lose our own vision. We are not the only ones who are grateful. God sees what we do for Him, and He is grateful.

T HERE IS AN OLD PROVERB:

As you walk through life
Let this be your goal.
Keep your eye on the donut,
Not on the hole.

Simple words, and profound! Our internal awareness really determines our attitudes, our level of happiness. If we look at what we have, what is there, we can be happy. If we look at what is not there, we are unhappy. So, look at the donut, not at the hole.

As we celebrate the Thanksgiving holiday, we try to muster up our gratitude. We have to look at the right thing. It is so strange that whatever we direct our attention to keeps getting bigger and bigger. If someone has a trait that irritates us and we keep looking at it, it grows and grows. In the end, we know nothing about this person except that one trait and it bugs us to death. What we look at grows. What we ignore shrinks. If we put all our energy into seeing what we do not have, we become truly deprived. If we keep our eye on what we have, we become richer and richer.

Happy Thanksgiving! I hope you have a lovely family celebration. I hope the gathering of your loved ones reminds you of how rich your life is. Then you and I can be ready to express our gratitude to God. I remind you that a good way to do that is at Mass on Thanksgiving Day. Moreover, I remind you of the proverbial wisdom:

Keep your eye on the donut,
Not on the hole.

WHEN YOU COME to the edge of the light, and are about to step off into the darkness of the unknown, faith is knowing one of two things will happen: There will be something to stand on, or you will be taught to fly.

You see a tightrope walker push a wheelbarrow across a tight wire. Faith is not believing he can do that. Faith is believing he can do it when you are in the wheelbarrow. Faith is not a detached belief. Real faith happens only when we are personally involved. There is no such thing as impersonal faith. In faith, we always take a personal risk.

Usually, when I make an act of faith and trust in God, it is based on my solution to the problem. If I am diagnosed with cancer, I try to firmly believe that God can and will cure cancer and that I will be well. But, it is possible that God has another solution to my problem. Rather than give me firm ground to stand on, God may want to teach me to fly. God's solution to my sickness may be to teach me to achieve greatness through the disease of cancer. Or God's solution may be to cure me. Faith means that I simply trust God, and His solution, not mine.

We are all believers. We are waiting for God to give us firm ground to stand on. Let us be true believers. We should not limit the range or the power of God. He may want to teach us to fly. So FLY!

I N MY LEXICON OF SAINTS, two people stand out, aside from those directly associated with the life of Christ. They are St. Francis of Assisi and St. John of the Cross. I would like to reflect on that second gentleman.

John was a Spanish Carmelite priest who died on December 14, 1591, just over 400 years ago. He was a co-worker and friend of the Carmelite Sister St. Teresa of Avila. They both spent their lifetimes reforming their orders. John was a little guy, less than five feet tall. (That is why I like him.) John seems to us today to be almost inhuman. He is so ascetic. He seemed to give up all the pleasures of life we so enjoy. Our first reaction is: "Who would want to be like him?" He scares people. He even scared St. Teresa, not exactly a lightweight herself.

Yet, John can teach us. He believed in pleasure. He did not run from material pleasure. He ran toward the pleasure God could give him. He became so overwhelmed with the pleasure of spirituality, he forgot about material things. He was too busy for material things; his mind was otherwise occupied. John figured we would all depend upon the presence of God to be happy in eternity. John decided he would start that process right here on Earth. If God can fill us with pleasure in eternity, He can do so right now. Why fool around with lesser sources of pleasure? John found that pleasure, he found ecstasy, and he found sainthood. In a very difficult and stressful life, no one was happier.

In our present day, the life of St. John of the Cross teaches and confronts us. Do we believe that God can make us perfectly happy? Do we believe He will if we look only to Him? St. John shows us the way and gives us hope. I cannot experience God to the extent St. John did (I don't think). Yet, I can experience God. He is waiting to give me this experience. We all can have this experience. Then when we experience this joy, maybe material things will not seem so important.

I F LOVE IS NOT taught in the home, it is difficult to learn anywhere else.

Some things in life must be done in the proper order. Loving is one of those things. We do not teach others to love in an intellectual way. It is not a classroom project. We teach people to love by loving them. It was meant that we would love our little people and then teach them this most important of all human skills.

Ideally, a person would never remember when or how he or she learned to love. Learning this fine art is just a natural part of life. Our parents love us from day one, and we naturally love them and each other. It seems to come naturally.

What if that very natural process does not happen? Then, a child would need "remedial loving" as some children need remedial reading. "Remedial loving" is a very difficult project. If you are not loved, it is all but impossible to become loving.

If we teach a child to love, then loving becomes a natural instinct. If love has to be a studied reaction, then, I am afraid, it never quite happens. Love does need to be a resolution. We do need to work at sensitivity. But if these qualities are not part of our natural make up, we may never make it.

Some things in life must be done in their proper order. I think our most important work of life is teaching children to love by loving them.

THIS WEEKEND, FR. DAVID will begin our parish mission. Fr. David is a member of the Spiritual Life Institute, a religious community of both men and women in the Carmelite tradition.

These monks believe in solitude and silence. First, solitude: They choose to experience large amounts of aloneness. They want God to identify them individually, so they spend time alone and quiet down all the other voices. They spend one day a week and one week a month in complete isolation. They see solitude as a unique access to God. Their community comes together only three times a week to celebrate Mass and eat together.

Then in their solitude, they embrace silence on a vast scale. Their way of life is one of silence, one of quiet attentiveness to the voice of God. If we are going to hear the voice of God, we must still all the noise around us. We all live in a world of noise. People take a walk in the woods and put on a Walkman, so as not to experience the silence.

Fr. David is here to tell us the benefits and the joys of silence and solitude. He will not turn any of us into monks. But solitude and silence can have a part in our life. We are not called to be monks, but we are called to be contemplative. We find out who we are when we experience our aloneness, and we find intimacy with God in silence. Fr. David can show us the way.

H OW DO YOU PRAY? Let us take a closer look at prayer, perhaps a new look. Prayer is an end in itself, not a means to something else. Prayer of petition is a long tradition in the church. The purpose of prayer is to commune with God, not to obtain something. I hear people talk about prayer like, "This prayer really works." Prayer is an end, not a means to something we want. I have a pamphlet in my office that guarantees that a certain prayer will get spirituality; this is just silly. The result of prayer is intimacy with God, no guarantees, no secret payoffs, no double green stamps on Wednesdays. Is not intimacy with God enough?

We can look on prayers as an experience, an adventure, and not just a duty. If we really spent time giving ourselves to God, He just might respond in some way. That experience would be an adventure. It does happen. It is possible. You do not have to be St. Francis of Assisi to experience God. Ordinary people have such experiences. (They just do not have them as Francis did!)

So, I ask: How do you pray? Does prayer enrich you? Is there excitement? Is it enjoyable? If we just spend time alone with God and just "be" in His presence, we might find enjoyment and sometimes excitement. How God gives Himself to each of us depends on God. If we give Him our time and our attention, He just might touch us in return. When that happens, prayer becomes an adventure. It happens to ordinary people — like us.

W E ALL HAVE a different emotional orientation in life. Some are optimists; some are pessimists. Some are angry; some are peaceful. One of the wonderful priests of our diocese reminds me of J.D. Salinger's "Paranoid in Reverse." He thinks that the whole world is plotting to make him happy. I would like to think about the angry people. I do identify with them.

One of my principles in life is that I am never angry at what I think I am angry at. There is always something deeper going on. The sign of this is when I overreact. A minor irritant becomes a major anger. Then I know that something else is going on.

When someone offends me by some thoughtless act and I go into a rage, what is going on? What I need to ask is when have I felt like this before? What is this reminding me of? Sometimes I can answer these questions and sometimes I cannot. I am angry about something in my past, not about this present moment. The person facing me must think I have lost my mind, going into such anger over some little thing. Some people are offensive, but they do not deserve all the anger I have been storing up for 10 years.

To be honest, angry people have to figure out whom they are really angry at. The only way out of anger is to forgive sincerely. When angry people get tired of carrying all the anger around, they must forgive. The angriest people I know do not forgive easily. They save up hurts and carry them around. When they want to get really angry, they get out the hurts and feel them all over again.

The answer is to forgive. We forgive, not for the benefit of those people, but for our own benefit. This does not happen until a person is sick of being angry. Letting go of anger is a boon to ourselves.

BEING THROWN INTO unaccustomed surroundings with unknown people can make any of us uncomfortable. However, it can be a very healthy experience. In such a situation, we tend to find out who we are. This experience forces us to draw on our own inner identity and inner strength to be comfortable. In a new situation, all the standard supports we depend on are gone.

A person starting a new job has this experience. So does anyone moving into a new neighborhood. Think of a young person going off to college. Even worse, think of a kindergartner's first day in school. This is more than uncomfortable. This is positively terrifying. Yet, look at how children blossom through this experience. This not only shows us who we are; it makes us who we are. The experience is a gift, granted a painful one.

As we go through adulthood, we tend to be able to avoid such experiences. We can get into a pattern in our lives and just keep going, nothing new, nothing scary, nothing challenging. Another word for this pattern is "rut." In my life, going to visit our sister parish in Honduras gives me this experience. I am in a different world. I cannot speak much of the language. I know nobody. No one knows me. I feel OK. I have to rely on what I find inside myself. I have found that a weeklong stay at a monastery or retreat house provides the same experience.

Are you open to such an experience? Many in our parish are giving serious thought to going to Honduras one of these years. Make it more than a nice thought or a good intention. As the Nike people say, "Just do it." You will hate it and love it at the same time. And you will grow. You will end up thanking God for the gift. It is not something you would do often. Once might just be enough.

A WISDOM SAYING: "One moment's acceptance of everything that is, is better than a thousand years of piety."

Wisdom sayings do not express truth; they express wisdom. They may not be true. For example: "A stitch in time saves nine." Sometimes, a stitch in time saves nothing. I would still bet on its usefulness. Example: "A penny saved is a penny earned," not with inflation. To save money is still wise.

I like the wisdom contained in the above statement. Acceptance of ugly reality is so hard for us. Acceptance does not mean we like the ugly reality or approve of it. Acceptance simply means that we can live with it. Acceptance is the secret of a happy life. There is so much wrong with the world. There is so much I do not like. But I will never be happy unless I accept the things I cannot change.

We all live with a lot that we do not approve of. We must because we simply cannot control what other people do. We have to live with these other people. If we cannot change others, we can change our own attitudes. We can work hard to change the bad in our world. Then we must accept what is.

God made an imperfect world. It is His world. If we want to blame anyone, we can blame Him. If we want to be close to God, we will get there with acceptance better than with piety. Can we ever accept everything that is? I think it is possible, but I do not think I have ever met anyone under 80 who has succeeded. So, there is hope!

REJOICE IN the Good News: God is unjust—he makes the sun shine on the good and the bad alike.

What a statement! It reminds me of the parable of the workers in the vineyard. In that story, the workers said that their employer was unjust. As fair-minded people, we rebel at the idea that God could be unjust. However, who of us desires to relate to God on a basis of justice with God? If we only get justice from God, we are all in trouble. Anyone who can look inside himself knows that we want mercy from God, not justice. We want friendship, love, and intimacy, not justice from God. Therefore, an unjust God is good news. A God who relates to us on some other basis than justice is good news.

Have you ever known a parent who was aware of exactly what he owed his child? If so, he was not much of a parent. We want to give our children not just their legal rights. We want to give all we have. That is what love does for us. To say that God is unjust is simply to say that our relationship with God is dominated by His love.

To say God is unjust is to say He loves us as individuals. He does not feel for us as a farmer feels for a herd of cattle. To the farmer, they are 100 heads. If they weigh the same, they are the same. They do not have names. He would treat them all the same.

The "Good News" is that you and I have names in the mind of God. We are not all the same. He does not treat us all the same. He is Father; we are beloved children.

Thus, the Good News: God is unjust.

W E COME TO THE beginning of the liturgical year of the church. The church recalls to our minds the long time of preparation for the coming of Christ. The Jews spent almost two millennia preparing themselves for the coming of Jesus.

We go through this memory every year to remind ourselves that our redemption is not complete. We are not where God wants us to be—yet. We are not what God wants us to be—yet. We have a ways to go for our redemption to be complete. That means that we are somewhat in the same position as those Jews waiting for the coming of Christ. We, too, are waiting for something.

It strikes me that one of the more startling ideas of Jesus was His understanding of human potential, our potential. He thought that we could attain God Himself as an intimate child. This is really a stretch for all of us. It is frightening. We would rather think that our task on earth was to keep the laws, to be just acceptable. Yet, Jesus thinks we can attain intimacy with God. Wow! That is a lot to look forward to. It is scary.

The season of Advent reminds us of our potential. We can be so much more than we are right now. Christ is still promising to come to us in more depth. Advent tells us this. The last sentence of the Bible says, "Come Lord Jesus." This very beautifully expresses the theme of Advent.

T HE JEWS HAD AN ELEMENT in their religion that, as far as I know, was unique in the history of religion. All religions remember and celebrate some past blessing from God. The Jews did something different. They did not remember, but they relived. The past blessings of God were not past. They were always present. The Jewish Exodus from Egypt was not past history. It was happening now. God did not lead our ancestors out of Egypt; He led us out of Egypt. The Passover Supper did not celebrate this past event. The Passover celebrated the fact that this liberation was still happening. This is a very different approach to a religious feast.

Christians adopted this approach to religious celebrations. We take this approach in every celebration of Mass. The Mass is not just a commemoration of the sacrifice of Jesus. We are doing more than just remembering. We believe that through the priesthood, Christ truly becomes present in the elements of bread and wine, present in His act of sacrifice. We are not just remembering; we are reliving. We participate in His act of giving and make it our own. We celebrate the Lord's Supper very much like the Jews celebrate Passover. The acts of God's goodness are not past; they are forever present.

As we approach Advent and Christmas, we do not say Christ came. We say He is coming. To us, the coming of Christ is always happening. We have not yet received the fullness of Christ's coming. It is still coming. We need to PREPARE.

DURING ADVENT, we recall the longing of the Jews for the promised Messiah. We try to put ourselves in their place and long for God to fill up our lives more completely. We are simply trying to make God real in our lives.

The fact is that God is trying to come into our lives. His coming was not completed in the first century. God is not finished with any of us yet. Our salvation is not finished. We are not perfected. God is coming to us at this Christmas just as He once did for the Jews. We celebrate Advent; we celebrate Christmas, to make this coming real to us.

We cannot let Jesus become a historical figure in our lives. We have many historical figures that we revere. Christ was born to us out of personal love for you, for me. George Washington was not. George's birthday was an important event in the history of our country. We celebrate it every year. It is history. December 25th is not just history. It is personal.

We have many heroes of our past. Christ is not one of them. Christ is not in our past; He is in our present. He is touching our lives now and He wants to touch our lives more. Christ did not come to us as a species; He comes to individuals. He is trying to come in a new way to each of us. This is what we celebrate. The better we celebrate the love God has for us, the more we make it happen.

May you and I be ready for the coming of Christ into our lives.

IF YOU FIND YOU REST in Jesus Christ, you will never know a moment's ease again. I think that this statement sounds horrible. Does it mean that we can never relax if we are Christians? Did not Christ Himself relax at times? I do think that the above statement is true, but it is not as bad as it sounds. I think that it means that we can never be content to stand still. We must always be on the move. God wants us to be perfect as He is perfect.

I fantasize that Christ is always calling us, "Come over here where I am." But when we get there, He is gone and He is still saying, "Keep coming with me." We can rest, but not for long. We are always on the journey following Jesus. It seems to me that the secret is to learn to enjoy the journey, so that you will not want to stop. Of course, we can rest, but never for long.

Christ has this incredible vision of each human person. He thinks that each of us is perfectible. To get to that perfection, we must keep moving. The ultimate betrayal of Jesus is to reach a point where we say to ourselves, "Enough! I am good enough. I do not need to change anymore. My journey is over." When we say this, we are denying everything that we are about.

If we take our ease in Jesus Christ, we will always hear His voice. His voice is forever saying, "You cannot stop there. I am over here." His voice tells us that the journey never ends.

I T IS TRUE that a person with big dreams is more powerful than one with all the facts. This is another way of saying that reality stinks. This is another way of saying that we must stretch reality by our dreams. This is another way of saying that every great achievement was once considered impossible.

In the play, "The Man of La Mancha," the Don Quixote character recalls being in prison and watching men die. He said that they died crying because they were in touch with reality, but they had no dreams. People said that Don Quixote was insane, out of touch with reality. Don Quixote said, "What is so great about reality? I would rather be in touch with my dreams."

I think that none of us can handle reality by itself. We must see what is, but we must also see what could be. We must hang on to our dreams. This is a theme of Advent. The season of Advent proclaims that something is always coming to us. If we are not dreaming, God is dreaming for us. If we get out of God's way, He will see that our dreams far outdistance our present reality.

So, let us dream in a healthy manner, because God is doing so. What we are is small potatoes compared with what we will be.

T HE FIRST INTERPRETATION of the meaning of Jesus comes at the beginning of St. Matthew's Gospel when he quotes the Prophet Isaiah, "The One born of a Virgin will be called Emmanuel, meaning God with us." Surprisingly, St. Matthew's Gospel ends on the same thought. As He ascends into heaven, Jesus says, "Behold I am with you always, until the end of time." Throughout, Jesus is "God with us."

Presence is a precious gift. We have all been moved in our past when we were facing some trial. A friend comes and says, "I am with you." A friend cannot usually fix us, but he or she can be with us. That makes a difference.

It is so incredible that God Himself would choose to be our partner as we go through the pains of life. His presence expresses that He cares, that He loves. The love of another human person does make such a difference in our lives. What can the love of God do, if we truly believe?

The message of the Gospel is that no problem is too much, because God is with us. No sickness can overcome us because, God loves us. Even death cannot overwhelm, because God has us by the hand.

God is with us, the Good News of Jesus Christ.

" THE WORD WAS MADE FLESH." One life can make a difference, any one life. We have seen what a difference the life of Jesus has made. Since His birth, the world has never been the same.

Does any one life make a difference? What about yours? What about mine? I am quite sure that none of us is going to change the course of history. We all know that we do indeed make a difference. We make a difference to our families. No one has ever had the effect upon us as our parents did. Parents make a huge difference in the lives of their children. I am not a parent. Many are not. We still can make a difference. We can touch other people and change lives.

I would like to think that when I die, I would leave a hole in the world around me. We would all like to leave a hole. We would like to think that we would be missed. We even have delusions of grandeur, where we dream how the world will be devastated without us. (Or am I the only person with such delusions?)

We are not necessary for the continuation of civilization. But we can leave behind a hole when we depart. We must make a difference. We must strive to see that the hole we leave behind is as big as possible.

"The Word Was Made Flesh." One life did make a difference. One life still can. I want that life to be mine. You want it to be yours. Let us make it so.

T HE GREAT FEASTS of the Christian year are Christmas, Easter, and Pentecost. Easter is usually considered the most sacred feast of our church year, and I would hesitate to disagree with that assessment. Christmas is by far the happiest feast. Christmas is the "warm fuzzy" of all church celebrations. On Easter, the ugly memory of Christ on the cross is still very fresh. On Christmas, we deal only with the child in the manger. We celebrate with unmixed joy.

We celebrate these events every year so that we may enter into them more fully, and it is pure joy to enter into the Christmas event. We recall that God loved us so much that He became one with all of us. This "happening" is far beyond our imagination. Who could have fantasized such an event? God did plenty for us by creation. That He would share our dependent condition with all its limitations and pain is something beyond anything we could imagine. The image of God doing this for us is the infant in the manger.

Who can resist a newborn baby? Not one of us could possibly be intimidated by such a child; even believing the child is God. God came to us in the most appealing form He could find. This is what we celebrate on Christmas. It is such a staggering event and such a happy surprise that words fail us.

To celebrate this event, we must do what we always have to do in the presence of the mystery of God. We must just be in the "Presence" of the mystery, and bask in the love. Just drink it in and our prayer may be just two words, "Thank You." I hope you take time at Christmas to experience the feast in front of the crib. Just drink it in!

T HE CHRIST CHILD presents all of us with an unforgettable image. We need to think about what this image really means to us. What does this image represent?

The more I get on with life, the more I realize that life involves almost a constant letting go of something. We are always being called upon to let go. I am inclined to say life is about letting go.

Leaving home to go to kindergarten may seem to us simple and routine, but to a child of five years, it is an enormous piece of "letting go." The child lets go of the security of home and enters into a new, scary world. At every stage of life thereafter, letting go is called for. I believe that we humans cannot make real progress toward maturity without letting go of something significant. I think it is a law of nature.

The Christ Child in the crib is an image of letting go. Never has there been such an act of letting go. "Jesus did not think being God something to be clung to but emptied Himself," Philippians 2. Going from Infinite God to man is quite a journey. Jesus became not just a man, but a human infant. It is hard to imagine a creature more helpless, more vulnerable than a human infant is. Jesus went from all-powerful God to helpless baby. We cannot imagine a greater letting go.

This is the image of Christmas, an image of God letting go of all to become one with us. It is an image of love. May you carry this image with YOU.

WHAT DO WE SEE in the crib? We see a newborn baby and we are thrilled. The child is pure potential. He or she could be the greatest President of the United States, (or he or she could be a very bad President of the United States). We cannot know, and so we think (and hope for) the best.

When Jesus was in the crib, God had become man. It was the greatest event in history. Yet, this baby Jesus was still potential. He could approach His mission in many different ways. Our reaction to this God-Man was also pure potential. We could react in a million different ways. We could rejoice in Him and love Him, or reject Him and even kill Him. The human race chose the worst possible option.

Yet, God's design still made the whole thing work. God's will "was" done. God took our worst of all possible choices and made something good out of it. God took our worst possible moment and turned it into a moment of grace. When we say that God is all-powerful, this is what we mean.

Let us remember! When we look into the crib, what do we see? We see God made man. We see the potential for much good and the potential for terrible evil. We see God undisturbed. God knew that the power of His love was enough to cover the worst of our reactions.

For this, we stand in awe in front of the crib, and we are grateful.

T HE FIRST TIME I spent Christmas totally away from family was in 1958. I was a theology student in Rome. I had arrived there a few months earlier. My first days in Rome were filled with excitement. Pope Pius XII died and Pope John XXIII was elected. Within a month, I had attended a Papal funeral, a Papal election, and coronation. I loved Rome, but I was not prepared for Christmas alone.

I have rarely been homesick, yet I could not believe how bad I felt. I kept thinking about home and family and felt worse and worse. I forced myself to celebrate Christmas in a traditional Roman way. I attended Mass at midnight in the North American College, at 5:00am in St. Cecilia's in the poor section of Rome, and at 8:00am in St. Peter's Basilica. This last mass was to be celebrated by a Cardinal. There were only about 200 of us in the massive St. Peter's. The assigned Cardinal turned out to be the new Pope.

Pope John the XXIII came walking out of the Sacristy all alone and walked to the main altar. He wowed everyone around. He quietly said, "I am going to have a quiet Mass. Please make the responses for me and help me celebrate." We did!

I do not often "hobnob" with Popes. That was the first time. (It was also the last time!) He was just like any other priest having Mass for a bunch of friends. Except he was the successor of Peter celebrating in a 400-year-old Basilica designed by Michelangelo! We did not get this sort of thing in Lansing, Michigan. I was homesick. I missed my family and my home, but during 8:00 o'clock Mass on December 25, 1958, I decided I could live with it.

T HERE ARE so many creative ways to celebrate the feast of Christmas. Various nations and cultures have their own beautiful way of remembering the Birth of the Savior. Families, too, can develop special ways of observing Christmas that can make a lasting impact on children. It would be wonderful if more families would develop their own unique customs of Christmas.

I have celebrated Christmas with a family of loved ones for more than 20 years. This family of 6 children developed a beautiful Christmas dinner tradition. The father would propose a question for us to discuss. We would often go on for 2-3 hours. I remember one Christmas when we were asked to name the quality of each person at the table, which we most appreciated. What a conversation that was! Some of the youngest children blew us apart.

As the children grew older, the discussions changed, but were even more fascinating. Now the adult children in the family propose the issue to discuss. But the custom is the same; all must address the issue. Last year when we celebrated, the subject was, "What are you most grateful for in the last year?" On that occasion, the parents and the priest in this family had to struggle to keep up with the "children."

This custom began for the benefit of the children. I do believe that now the children are continuing the custom for the benefit of the three older people. And I, for one, do benefit.

This Christmas, I will be with them and we will continue our tradition. I suspect this year we will talk about Ryan Patrick, the first grandchild born about a month ago. We all have much to learn from each other because of this event. I am sure that within four years, Ryan Patrick will be making his own contribution to the discussion, enriching elders, as his mother did 20 years ago. I can't wait!

"A VIRGIN SHALL bring forth a son and he shall be called Emmanuel which means God with us." Isaiah 7, 14.

Jesus is not just a part of history like all the other events. Jesus is the "Event" around which all history revolves. Jesus was born into the world, not from the world. He did not evolve out of history; He came into history from the outside. Jesus is not man becoming God, but God becoming man from the outside. Jesus' birth was an advent to human people.

On the first Christmas, Jesus came to the human race. We have to see that this becomes a personal advent. Jesus has come to the human race; has He come to me? That is a personal issue that depends upon my opening myself to the coming of God. This is a task of our prayer.

We do not usually let God in on any one occasion. It could happen, but I think the process of letting God in takes a lifetime. It is a task of prayer. Day by day, when we pray, we ask God to be born in us. We reduce our ego and make room for God.

Every year when we celebrate the feast of Christmas, we do so to open ourselves more to God. As we think about His birth and celebrate with joy, Jesus is born within us more fully and continues to take over our lives. The birth of Jesus was not just a historical event. We must make it personal, to me - to you.

CHRISTMAS IS A FEAST of God's love. However, so is Easter; so is Good Friday. But Christmas is a feast of pure joy, the revelation of God's love. On Good Friday, we cannot help but feel a bit guilty about God's love. As we remember the death of Jesus, we must recognize that we have not received that love very well. On Easter, we are still filled with that awareness. But on Christmas, we feel only the joy of God's love.

If there were no Jesus, and no Bible, I believe that we could know that there is a God. We could conclude there is a God just from observing creation. But what kind of a God would we know about? I believe that we would have to conclude that God created out of love and then left us to make the best of His creation. I believe that we would conclude that God was very, very distant and very cold. Without Jesus Christ, we could know God the creator, but we would never know the God of Loving Providence.

This is our Christmas present from God. God did not just love us in creating, but He loves us in His Providence for us. His love continues through every step of our existence.

St. Paul in writing to the Philippians said it best:

"His state was divine, yet he did not cling to his equality with God but emptied himself to assume the condition of a slave, and became a man as we are."

The love of the God of Jesus did not stop with creation but continues to touch us every day. The image of the Christ-infant in the crib carries that message. Christmas is a feast of pure joy. Let us celebrate.

I FOUND A LETTER from a Franciscan Friar, which beautifully expresses a New Year's wish. Fra Giovanni, an unknown Franciscan in 1513 AD, wrote this. That was four years before Martin Luther nailed his "95 Theses" to the church door in Wittenberg. The letter speaks for itself:

I salute you. I am your friend and my love for you goes deep. There is nothing I can give you which you have not got; but there is much, very much, that, while I cannot give it, you can take.

No Heaven can come to us unless our hearts find rest in today. Take Heaven! No peace lies in the future which is not hidden in this present little instance. Take Peace! The gloom of the world is but a shadow. Behind it, yet within our reach, is Joy. There is radiance and glory in the darkness, could we but see-and to see we have only to look. I beseech you to look.

Life is so generous a giver. Welcome it, grasp it, and you touch the Angel's hand—it brings it to you. Everything we call a trial or a sorrow, a duty, believes me, that Angel's hand is there; the gift is there, and the wonder of an overshadowing presence. Our joys too: be not content with them as joys. They, too, conceal diviner gifts.

Life is so full of meaning and purpose, so full of beauty beneath its covering—that you will find earth but cloaks your heaven. Courage then to claim it, that is all! But courage you have, and the knowledge that we are pilgrims together, wending through unknown country, home.

And so, at this Christmas time, I greet you. Not quite as the world sends greetings, but with profound esteem and with the prayer, that for you, now and forever, the day breaks, and the shadows flee away.

CONSIDER THE UPCOMING YEAR. What kind of a year will it be? Will it be a good year for you? Will it be a great year? Will it be the best year of your life so far? Could you make it so?

I think a year is too much time to look at. Let us consider one day. When was the last time you had a great day? I hope it was yesterday. When you had a great day, did you notice? Or did it slip by unnoticed? One of those days in our past was the best we have ever had. Did we notice that? Or did the best day of our life slip by? It is shocking to think that we could live the best day of our life and not even know it.

What if our best day comes in this coming year? Will we notice? What would we do to make sure we noticed? What if we woke up each day during the next year, and said a prayer of thanks to God for the gift of that day. If we considered each day a gift from God, I really do suspect we might notice when we had a great day. What if we began each day with that level of awareness? Then we would be ready for the best day of our life.

I do hope our best day is still ahead of us. I hope we can all live looking forward and not backward. Most of all, I hope that when that "best day" comes, we will notice.

DO YOU KNOW anyone who is comfortable with not carrying a watch of some kind? I do not. I am most certainly not comfortable without a watch. I am always in a hurry to keep the next appointment. I do like to be on time. I live by the clock. Without a watch, I am disoriented. I think we are obsessed with time in our society. We celebrate New Year's as a significant passage of time.

It is difficult for us to imagine that some people did not live by the clock but lived by the events of nature. For example, a friend of mine was traveling in China and his tour took him to see cottage industries. They went into a home where twenty women were putting together toys. He asked, "How many of these can you make in a day?" They answered, "That depends upon the day. Days in the summer are longer than days in the winter." They stared at each other; surprised that he would not know that. Some people do not live by the clock.

In the Middle Ages, my guess would be that the majority of the population not only did not know what time it was, but did not know what year it was. I suspect they could not have cared less. For most of them, I suspect, the struggle of life was so difficult, they could only take it a day at a time. They did not tend to look down the road, or at the calendar.

Our obsession with time is of recent vintage historically. It could be an advantage for us. We could be obsessed with the idea that time is a gift. If we got into every day with some intensity, if we thanked God for each day, then our obsession with time would make us grateful people.

Happy New Year! This year hang on to your watch. Time reminds us of God's gift. Have a good year.

F OR SOME YEARS now, I have gone through a certain ritual at the end of the year. A close friend visits me and we review the year. I review my year, and she reviews hers. We look at where we have made progress and where we have failed. The process is rather like a two-way confession. We talk about the things we would like to achieve during the coming year. We make personal plans to make progress during the coming year. Of course, the achievement we seek is within us.

I find this year-ending ritual to be very healthy for me. I wish I could say it was my idea, but it was not. My friend came up with the idea. This ritual helps me focus on where I am in my journey to God and where I am going.

We are building something in life and what we are building is inside us, our character. It is the only thing we can build that will last. The character we build will last forever. I want to be ambitious in this building project.

I used to think about what I wanted to achieve in life. We can only do what we can imagine. We only achieve what we can dream about. My friend does me a real favor by giving me an occasion to do some serious thinking at the end of each year. This ritual is my version of the New Year's resolution. I recommend it.

T HERE IS A SAYING that has been rather helpful to me. It says, "It is never too late to have a nice day." What this really says is that we can always start over. It is never "too late" to start over. If you are having a bad morning, you can always decide to start the day over again at noon and have a good day.

Starting over is very basic to personal growth. On our journey into God, we often are sidetracked. To make progress, we must start over all the time. Some people start that journey every day and find excitement in it. Some children act as if every day were the first day of creation. Starting over is a very healthy way to live.

This is what we traditionally do at the end of a year, or the beginning of a year. We start over. We resolve to live a richer life. We can make fun of New Year's resolutions, but it is hard to see how anyone could make progress without some resolve to do so. I hope that all of us hold out for ourselves the possibility that each New Year may be our best year ever. It could be our best year, not because of externals like winning the lottery, but because our insides are at peace, because we possess happiness from within. Only God gives that kind of happiness.

This New Year might be our best year ever. It is a real possibility. May we resolve to make it so. May we be open to the happiness within that God wants to give.

On January 1, we can start over. In the days before that, we can remember that it is never too late to have a good year.

WHEN I WAS YOUNG, I dreamed of living until the year 2000. I knew that in that year, I would become 65 years of age. I thought that I would be too old to enjoy the event, but it is here and I am not too old. I am overjoyed to be here and now.

If you are reading this, it means that the end of the world did not come at the midnight of Friday night. I hope by this time we know how much of a problem Y2K is going to be. Now we can figure out how we feel about a new Millennium.

I think that the second Millennium was way ahead of the first as far as progress was concerned. A good two centuries of the first Millennium were called the Dark Ages, not without reason. The fall of the Roman Empire occurred before that. It was the biggest political collapse in human history, and it brought a century of chaos before and after. The first Millennium was pretty rough.

The second was better, but it was no bargain. One war lasted 117 years; another 30 years. Throw in the four years of the Black Death, and you do not have a walk in the park. However, there was progress. Certainly there was material progress. Planes, cars, phones, computers, and televisions all make life a lot easier, at least in a material way.

I think that progress must be measured in terms of mans relations. In our century, a man arose who said that political objectives can be achieved by nonviolent means. Then he did it. Something new entered human history. As we enter the third Millennium, there is a great hunger for inner spiritual development. There is concern for ecology, for our world and its future. And Shakespeare and Mozart are alive and well.

The human race may show its true mettle in this next Millennium. I hope we see progress in terms of our learning to love each other. The pace of life will quicken. I hope the pace of true progress will quicken.

I RECENTLY ATTENDED the "Pastor's Convention" which we hold every year in Ann Arbor, Michigan. It is held not only for priests but also for all in pastoral ministry. We had 190 participants. The leader threw some good questions at us.

Where is the scarcity in your life? What are you lacking? What is in short supply? Of course, the answers might be material things. I imagine everyone is a bit short on cash. However, I would bet that the most important shortages in our lives are of a nonmaterial nature. We all crave intimacy and as much as we want intimacy, we are afraid of it. Is peace of mind in short supply? Or excitement, or wisdom, or tolerance, or patience? We get to an age where energy is in short supply for all of us. What would it take to make you happier? What scarcity do we really need a cure for to be happy?

In the midst of scarcity in our lives, where do we find abundance? What do we have going for us? What do we thank God for? As we get older and lose energy, I hope we get smarter. Less energy and more wisdom is a good bargain. One of the things I like about getting older is that I do not have to work so hard to have a good time. Maybe that just means that I am getting boring. Whatever it is, I like it.

If we ask, "What do I need to be happier?" We should also ask, "What is making me happy now?" I would be willing to bet the answer is right under our noses. The elements in our life that give the most happiness may be the things we most take for granted. Hence, the importance of the question.

SEVERAL YEARS AGO, we had another terrible earthquake in Mexico City. The next day I met a priest friend named George for lunch. That day, George was not himself. He did not feel like eating. He was withdrawn and did not want to explain himself. Finally, he came out with the problem.

George was upset because, he said, "There is a man buried in the rubble in Mexico City. Today, he is going to realize that rescuers will not find him, and he will give up hope. Tomorrow he will die. He is in pain."

I asked if he knew this man personally. He said, "No, of course not. But he is real. I feel for him."

In recent years, Popes have spoken to us frequently of solidarity. That simply means that we humans are all one family and we should feel that conviction. We are all brothers and sisters and we should act accordingly. There is no longer "us" and "them." We are all one family.

At that lunch a few years ago, my friend George gave me a super lesson in solidarity. The unity of the human family was not an idea taught by George. He felt it. He was truly related to that suffering man in Mexico City. They were brothers. George was some piece of work. A few years later, George followed his friend into eternity.

Each year, part of our family is devastated by earthquakes. I hope we all feel their suffering, their fear. I hope we are always generous in sending our material support to those suffering. Solidarity is for realizing we have one and the same Father. We are family.

A FEW YEARS AGO, there was a news report that tickled me. A fast food operation in California served tainted meat and had managed to poison a number of their customers, several hundred as I remember. A few weeks later, the news release stated that the fast food business was changing its advertising firm, to project a more positive image. They did not mention anything about changing their meat supplier! This is one of those "Has someone lost their mind?" stories. I did love it. I laughed all week.

Our society is often more impressed by image than substance. We can all choose style over substance, and, I am afraid, all too often, we do so choose. One of our deceased priests was, in my opinion, the wisest priest we have ever had in our diocese. Yet, in his old age, people did not want to attend his Mass. He read his homilies, and he spoke in a monotone. He did not often tell stories. Yet, I never heard him say anything without some wisdom in it. He was a monument to substance over style. He was not popular.

In my vocabulary, to call someone a person of substance is a high compliment. It is to say that they are the "real thing." If anyone can become an authentic individual and maintain their own values, they have accomplished much in life. If a person is his own man, her own woman, that person is a person of substance. It does not matter what kind of clothing they wear. (There is no sartorial section in the Sermon on the Mount.)

So, a certain tennis player, filled with the vigor of youth, appeared on TV and said, "Image is everything." (Maybe the mental vigor will come later on.) Sorry. Image is not everything. It is not even close.

I T IS IMPORTANT to hang around the right people. If we want to get skilled at tennis, we need to play someone better than we are. If we want to become wise, we had better hang around some "good heads." We cannot become "growthful" people if we surround ourselves with those dedicated to stagnation.

It is so easy for all of us to get into our rut and rarely meet anyone who challenges us. God's greatest gift to us is people who help us take a step forward. Such people can make us uncomfortable, because they shake us out of our rut. It is always uncomfortable to change. Imagine what St. Francis of Assisi did to those around him. He drove them wild! He challenged people to live with different values. His goodness was inspiring, but frightening. Christ Himself was known to frighten a few people in His own day.

I think our greatest spiritual danger is stagnation, not falling into huge sins. We get too tired for all that heavy sinning. But we do love to float along in our comfortable rut. Once in a while God sends someone into our lives who shakes us up and gets us going again. That is His gift to us.

When was the last time such a person came into our lives? Did we recognize that person as a gift? Is there someone like that in our life right now? Do I recognize? When the next one comes along, will he recognize that gift?

It is very important to hang around the right people in life, and recognize who they are.

TODAY, WE ARE INVITING people to our church who have expressed some interest in the Catholic church. We will meet in church, I will show people around, and talk about what I think is special about my church. This makes me do some thinking. This is what I would propose for you today: If you were to play host this evening yourself, what would you say is special to you about our church?

All sorts of questions come to mind. What do you most enjoy about our church? What is most important to your personal growth? If you were to try to interest someone in the church today, what would you present to them?

What I greatly value in my religion is our approach to public worship. In our Mass, we are not just praying to God. In our readings, we are not just learning about God. In our Mass, we are striving to have an experience of God. We try to feel God's presence among us. We believe God is here. We have faith. We try to feel that reality. Our church building is designed to facilitate this experience. It is kept darker inside. We have stained glass windows. We have candles and paintings and sometimes incense. This helps to create an atmosphere in which we can more readily lift our minds to the Lord. We are trying to experience God.

An experience of God pretty much depends upon God. He reveals Himself to us as He wills. We just cannot decide that we are going to have an experience of God and then make it so. But we can get ourselves ready for such an experience if God would care to offer Himself.

We strive for such experience. We will spend eternity with this experience of God. In the Catholic church, we know that God often offers Himself right here and now. In our church, we strive for that experience. This approach is what I most value about our religion.

I T IS POSSIBLE for us to reduce religion to moralizing. All we have to do is forget about the great mysteries of God and the mystery of ourselves.

Priests can do this by constantly moralizing in homilies. A friend of mine told me about his pastor who repeated four themes. One was on church discipline and three were on sex. His constant themes: It is a sin to miss Mass on Sunday, to have sex outside of marriage, to practice birth control, and to have an abortion.

It is laudable to encourage people to live a moral life, but there is more to religion than that. In religion, we explore the wonder of God and prepare ourselves to share that wonder for all eternity. This is where religion gets deep, and becomes more than a rulebook. God is more than lawgiver. He is Infinite Mystery, Infinite Love and Compassion

We respond to God's love by morality. However, we need to go beyond the law. We need be comfortable with the mystery of God and rest in that Mystery. This is what our religion can do for us; it can enable us to encounter the real God. That is the ultimate experience. If each of us were in that kind of contact with God, we would be mystic people. Morality would naturally follow.

I N THE 1950'S, a famous priest had suffered near martyrdom in China. I heard him speak once. He was marvelous and inspiring. Twenty years later, I heard that he had died. Other priests of his order told me his real story. He was truly a martyr in China in the early 1950's. He survived and later allowed his order to make him their resident martyr. He made appearances and told his story repeatedly. He inspired. He was admired. He did no pastoral work, no confessions, no weddings, no funerals, no teaching. He was simply their resident martyr. By the time of his death, this wonderful man had become a colossal bore to his fellow priests. He had become a one-dimension person.

We are all, at least briefly, one-dimensional at times. You wake up with a stiff neck. You become a person with a stiff neck, period. Your malady overwhelms your self-awareness. By evening, you feel a bit better and you become a person with a stiff neck who likes golf, loves his children, and is crazy for the Beatles.

New brides and grooms, new parents, people in therapy, recovering alcoholics, all face the danger of being one dimension people for a while. People who become suicidal are always one-dimensional. They can only be aware of their pain. People who become "plaster saints" are always one-dimensional. They cannot afford to let the more questionable facets of life muddy the image of sanctity.

We cannot let ourselves become one dimension people. God made us with so many facets. To expose only one would be a shame. It would make each of us boring, no matter what dimension we care to show.

In "Don Quixote" Sancho said, "We are all as God made us, and some of us worse." Whether better or worse, we must be what God made. God intends no one dimension person.

G OD GIVES US two gifts: truth and repose. You have to choose one. You can never have both.

I came across this little jewel in my reading. As it applies to me, it is on target. I do not know about you. The problem with truth and repose, it seems to me, gets back to human nature or Original Sin, if you will. We are flawed human beings. If we face that truth, we must keep moving, keep changing. There is little time for R & R. When we say, "To heck with it, I am just fine as I am," then we can rest. However, we are no longer looking at facts.

Truth or repose? 'Tis a dilemma! I think what most of us do is try to have both. We choose repose and float along. We forget about truth for the time being. Then something causes truth to raise its ugly head, and we face it and get moving. Of course, if we get used to repose, we stand in danger of never letting truth into our consciousness again. We just float home. Growth stops. Before long we would not recognize truth if it fell in our laps. Not a pretty state!

People we call saints are those who never turn their back upon truth. They will tolerate no repose in their journey toward God. They are driven; they are insistent; they are generous. They simply cannot seem to be happy in repose. The magnetism of truth is too strong for them.

What are you currently choosing, truth or repose? I hope we are choosing truth. I hope I never let avoiding truth be a way of life for me — or for you. We want to make sure that our ventures into the land of repose are temporary and brief.

S T. JOSEPH PARISH, especially the pastor, lost a friend a while back. Fr. Stan came so close to death so many times and then recovered, that many of us presumed he could keep doing it. He could not! After 90 years, his heart finally gave out.

Fr. Stan touched the lives of so many. He lived here in retirement for 25 years, and he never stopped being a priest. Fr. Stan always wanted to do as much ministry as he could. He was not at all happy with me when I would not schedule him for daily Mass in church. He did not wish to retire from ministry.

I suspect that we at St. Joseph may have received the best years of his ministry. After he withdrew from being a pastor, he could be more relaxed. We saw Fr. Stan in his relaxed years when his kindly heart could shine forth. He could be so relaxed with children. They loved him, and he loved them.

He touched so many, and he touched me. I saw Fr. Stan as a truly mature man. He had grown old with grace. He had many definite ideas as to how the church should be, how the world should be. In his old age, he did not need to argue about such issues. He had no need to be proven right. Such issues of ego were behind him. He could and did relax. He showed me how a man can grow old with grace. I did not miss the lesson. I loved him for it.

We would all like to teach our loved ones how to grow old gracefully, how to approach death with faith and courage. We only get one chance to do that. Fr. Stan used his well.

I N ALL OF MY STUDY of the great mystics in our Catholic tradition, one thing stands out. All of these mystics were very aware of their own individuality, their distinctiveness. God especially called each one in a way different from every other human being. Each was INDIVIDUAL. What we all need to wake up to is the fact that each one of us is so created and so called. Mark Twain once said, "If you have to get to the age of 70 by another man's road, don't go." Mark Twain was not a mystic, but I am sure they would have liked him.

The Catholic church proposes saints to us, but not that we might just copy them. We can learn from them, but we must internalize their lessons, and still be ourselves. God in heaven already has one St. Francis. He does not need another one of him. He needs one of you, or me. We are not called by God to be anyone else.

The great mystics were not special because they had a unique call from God. We all do. These mystics were special because they pursued their individual call with ferocity. They refused to be anyone but who they were. We say that we enjoy our individuality, but I fear we also enjoy being one of the crowd. When God says to us, "Were you as good as you could have been?" we can say, "No, but I was better than Louie!" But that will not do. God wants "ME." The only valid comparison is to compare what I am with what I could be.

The great mystics knew who they were. They were giants of individuality. May we be the same? As St. Francis put it, "I have done what was mine to do; may Christ teach you what you are to do."

T HE GREAT CHALLENGE of life is to decide what is important and to disregard everything else.

To make the above decision sounds so easy, but we all have a problem with it, especially, I think, men. We can mouth all the right answers, but our actions take us in a different direction. For example, I know men who loudly proclaim that their children are the most important factor in their lives, yet they work 90 to 100 hours a week. They do so by choice. They do not have to work such hours. Who is kidding whom? For example, I know priests who say they love the priesthood so much, and yet they spend most of the time on administrative matters, material things. Who is kidding whom?

In the Star Wars movie, "The Phantom Menace", the Jedi Knight hero had a great line. Before going into battle, he advised his apprentice, "Maintain your focus. Your focus will determine your reality." I was astonished by the wisdom of this line. Decide what is important and disregard the rest. If something is really important, you must keep your eye on it. Your focus will determine your reality. Your children are the most important reality in your life, only if you keep your focus on your children.

We cannot just be in favor of everything that is good. We must have priorities. If we put all our energy in one direction, we cannot help but take energy away from another direction. The principle of Sir Isaac Newton: For every action, there is a re-action in an equal and opposite direction. We have to decide where our efforts in life are going to go, and where they are not going to go.

Maintain your focus. Your focus will really determine what is going on around you.

A MULE DRESSED IN a tuxedo is still a mule. This is a wisdom saying. It says that working on our outside is not enough. In "My Fair Lady", the misogynist, Henry Higgins, describes women: "Straightening up their hair is all they ever do. Why can't they straighten up the mess that's inside?" This, I think, applies more to men than to women. But, of course, not in my case, at least not as far as the hair is concerned. However, male or female, we need to do more than dress up our outsides.

The wisdom saying limps in one spot. We cannot change what we are. A mule is always a mule. He can be a great mule, but he will never be a racehorse. I think that there is not much difference between a poor mule and a great one. A mule does not have that much potential.

That is where human beings are so different. We have so much potential. Think of the difference between Joseph Stalin and John of the Cross. The first could not feel for others; he was a monster. The second touched the face of God. John did not get there by combing his hair or wearing better clothes. Our outsides do not bring out our potential.

Our whole culture speaks of the superficial. Advertisements tell us that we must look right, smell right, dress right, and talk right. We rarely hear that we must think right, be right. Our culture says it might not be so bad to be a mule, if you had a tuxedo. I think it would stink. Our culture stresses the outside. Our religion stresses the inside. Remember about the mule.

In AA we say, "Sober up a moron and in the end, all you have is a sober moron." A dubious improvement!

I F YOU COULD BE BRILLIANT or pleasant, which would you choose?

I would think that the choice would depend on who you are. If you are the President of the United States, I would hope you pick brilliant. I really do not care if our President is nice. I just hope he is bright. The polls of 1998 seemed to indicate that many of us felt that way.

But if you are an ordinary person like most of us, I would hope you would choose pleasant. Pleasant people tend to be happy. I am not so sure of brilliant people. One of the most memorable people I have ever known was our school janitor when I was a kid. He was pleasant all the time, because he was happy all the time. He was an Italian immigrant with no education. I do not think he was smart, but he was more fun to be around than anyone I knew. He was a legend in Lansing during the 1940's.

We tend to think that brilliance changes the world but kindness gets lost. Brilliance did give us the polio vaccine and the computer chip. It also gave us the Hiroshima Bomb and the B2 bomber.

Kindness does change the world. It gives us a world that is a quality place. Pleasant people enrich our lives. They teach us. I do believe we really learn only under the influence of love and gentleness. Pleasant people make themselves happy and certainly make others happy.

In the Old Testament, Solomon asked God for Wisdom. I do not mean to rewrite history. However, I will bet many wished that he had chosen pleasantness, kindness.

WHEN SOMEONE gives you free tickets, do not complain about the show.

The best free show we have is life itself. It is a gift. We simply were on the receiving end. The gift was not given at our birth. It was given today; it will be given again tomorrow. And we receive and receive. We can get so used to the gift, we forget it is a gift. When we seem to receive some big favor from God, like getting a good job, we are especially grateful. However, the everyday gift, we fail to notice.

The task of spirituality is to get ourselves in the frame of mind where we notice the gift. Real spirituality leads to awareness, to gratitude. God has given us a free ticket to life. Let us not complain when we occasionally have to wait in line to enjoy life's benefits. It is a free show. Let us enjoy. Let us be grateful.

"HOW WONDERFUL IT IS that nobody needs to wait a single moment before starting to improve the world." A young girl in her attic prison in Amsterdam wrote these words. Her name was Anne Frank.

What an extraordinary person Anne Frank was. For over two years, she hid in that attic with her family. She was so young. Any normal person would be planning to grow up and become free, and then begin to change the world. Anne Frank was anything but normal. She knew that she need not wait to improve the world. She could improve her world today. In writing her diary, she made all of our worlds different for us. In this, she was like St. Therese of Lisieux. We would know nothing of either, had they not written their books.

Our world is so full of people who are planning to change the world. They are simply waiting for the right time. I do believe that I must include my name in this group. We wait and wait and the right moment never comes, and we never make our contribution to the improvement of our world.

Anne Frank had it right. Opportunities to serve people surround us. The right time is now. If we do not do it today, possibly we never will. We do not need to wait. There is a corollary of this that I find interesting. We are all waiting to be happy. We think happiness will someday, somehow come to us. According to Anne Frank's theory, we cannot wait. If we cannot find a way to be happy today, we may never be happy at all.

Always, the time is now.

EVERY HUMAN BEING, I suspect has some kind of an image of God. Even an atheist has some idea of what God is like. He formulates an idea of God then rejects that God. No one has an adequate image of God. We cannot grasp what infinity is. However, some images of God are better than other images.

I am thinking along these lines because I attended a workshop for priests on "Various Images of God." The seminar was in New Orleans, Louisiana. (It was rough duty last week!) In this workshop, we examined various images of God that come from our Christian tradition, as well as other religions of the world. This was very interesting to me. Some religions thought of God as fearsome; we needed to protect ourselves against Him. In these religions, worship was a means of appeasing God, buying Him off.

Then we come to the image of God that Christ gave us in the 15th chapter of St. Luke. The Parable of the Prodigal Son presents a God who is beyond our dreams. This Father of Jesus Christ is concerned only about loving His children. After showering His love, He patiently waits for a response. In our seminar last week, we did not come across an image of God to compare with that of Jesus. However, other world religions were rich in imagery of God. It does help to see how other cultures view God.

Each one of us has our own personal image of God. Some images are better than others. Some images can be downright sick. It is so essential for each of us to carry a truthful image of God. If we read Luke 15 properly, we realize that there may be many things in life to be afraid of, but God is not one of them.

I ATTENDED A WORKSHOP in early January. Three bishops formed a panel to discuss the topic of the workshop. I mentioned to one of the priests how impressed I was with one of the bishops. The priest was from the bishop's diocese, and he agreed. But he said, "My bishop is more impressive here than at home." He went on to say that all the details of administration in the diocese seem to diminish him. He then added, "It happens to all of us."

This was one smart priest. "It happens to all of us." If we are caught up with the small details of life, we become diminished. The slogan says, "We are what we eat." It might be better to say, "We become what we worry about." If we occupy our life with small worries, we become small people. The art is to keep a proper perspective.

I remember being in a small group discussion when one of our members came in all stressed out. His new car had received a scratch. He was in crisis. The whole group jumped on him. Someone said, "Are you aware that in our country there are babies who went to bed hungry last night?"

The art is to keep a proper perspective. We can get so upset by a spot on the carpet, being 5-minutes late, slow traffic. The world does not turn on such issues. And babies do go to bed hungry. If we must worry, we need to worry about the right things. We cannot let small details diminish us. Or, as one of our bishops would say, "Don't sweat the small stuff."

SOME PEOPLE ARE SO GIFTED that we have to think God is unfair. Why give so much to this person and so little to me? As we all know, life is not fair. Some people seem just naturally good, kind, sympathetic, or generous. This too is a gift from God. When great talent and great goodness come in the same person, then God has a piece of work.

When I was a campus minister at Western Michigan University and Kalamazoo College in the 1970's, I knew a person like that. He taught Philosophy at K College. He was brilliant. He was wise. He was also helpless as far as the details of life are concerned. He usually forgot appointments. It was part of his charm.

I do not think I ever heard this wonderful man say anything that did not have some wisdom to it. He was always kind and sensitive to others. He did not need to "show off" his knowledge to anyone. His competence was obvious. He tried not to talk over our heads. This was no small feat for him. His wisdom was common sense wisdom. We could all identify with his wisdom. One did not need an IQ of 140 to understand his wisdom.

Twenty years later, I still remember my friend. So does a generation of Kalamazoo College students. God is not fair. He gave this professor more than the rest of us. But this man used his gifts for he was a gift. God did not give us his talents, but He gave him to us. Twenty years later, I am still tickled by my friend, and still grateful.

GOD GAVE US THE power to imagine. Without imagination, I suspect that Thomas Edison would have been a common laborer. He could not have invented anything unless it was first born in his imagination. Hence, the slogan, "Everything is created twice." It is created first in the mind, and again in reality.

This principle also applies in the creation of ourselves. We cannot become anything until we can imagine it. We cannot become what we cannot imagine. We need to put our imagination to work for our personal growth. We cannot become tolerant people without first seeing ourselves in our own mind being tolerant, or kind, or patient, or whatever.

We can, and must, use our imagination as a tool of our spiritual growth. We can look down the road and see what or who we would like to be at age 60, 70, or 80. I can imagine myself being like that. I will never get there unless I do imagine myself in that way. You and I have to be created twice. Once in our mind, and once in reality. God is behind both creations.

Let your imagination go wild. If you imagine yourself composing music like Beethoven, or painting like Van Gogh, you might want to do a reality check on yourself. To imagine yourself as heroically kind or incredibly sensitive is not unreal. We can all get there, but we can only become what we can imagine.

OUR MASS WAS MEANT to be a profoundly deep experience of God, a communal experience done by all of us together. How do we do it right? It is almost a silly question. We have never done it right and never will. How do we approach God? We do not; we cannot. The closer we get, the further away we are. But God can approach us. And it is my firm conviction that God wants to, both in our personal prayer and in our communal Liturgy. God does this; we do not. How do we make ourselves approachable? That is the pertinent question.

We make ourselves approachable by being awake, by being alert, and receptive. I find that for me, this takes energy. I cannot just go to Mass and take my seat. I have to bring energy to the celebration and be as conscious of the presence of God as I possibly can. Especially as the priest, I have to bring energy because I am not sitting in the pew. This is a communal effort to be alert. We all must bring energy. And we must bring faith.

I think it would help if we believe that God wants to come to us. He will do so in His own good time. He is on His own timetable, not ours. He will come when He chooses. Our job is to be ready when He does.

We must escape from the evil so often condemned in the Old Testament. That is the practice of empty ritual. We cannot let ourselves just go through the motions. Empty rituals are deadly. "You worship Me with your lips, but your heart is far from Me." When we bring energy, we make our rituals alive. As one who stands at the altar, I must do that. As one who sits in the pew, so must you. When God comes, He must find us ready. The New Testament ends with the words, "Come Lord, Jesus." We must make these our own words as we celebrate.

MARCUS AURELIUS was a Roman who lived in the 20th century. His day job was to be Emperor of the Roman Empire. But the work he loved was thinking. He was a Stoic philosopher. The Stoics were practical thinkers. They did not gaze at the stars. They tried to figure out how one could be happy in life. Marcus Aurelius was a good head. He once said that the art of living is more about wrestling than about dancing.

I find this statement striking. I am not even sure that I agree with it, but I am sure that there is much wisdom in the statement. It might well be engraved on every wedding invitation, every graduation diploma, every job application. I really hope for all of us that we do more dancing in life than wrestling, but I would not bet too much money on that thought. We are happy or sad in life depending upon our expectations. We would be wise to hope for celebration in life, but to be prepared for struggles.

We could all give a good listen to old Marcus. We do not even have to lower our expectations in life. But we must be prepared at any moment to accept that Marcus was right. Struggle can raise its ugly head at any time. (I am beginning to sound "Irish.")

Christ went a step beyond Marcus Aurelius in the Paschal Mystery. He said that if life is more about wrestling than dancing, that is not all bad. Christ thought that happiness came through struggling.

Celebration comes by rising above the pain in life. Marcus Aurelius is worth listening to. Much more so is Jesus Christ.

THE TRIP IS OFTEN more important than reaching the destination. We have all experienced the truth of the above statement. Our education was far more important than our diploma. I once knew the CEO of a moderately large company. He knew his job necessitated a good-looking bottom line. He had to make money. However, he considered his real job was to work with people. His real job was to put people together in a creative way, so that each one could best use their talent. This daily exercise was more important to him than the bottom line.

The Medieval Pilgrimage was like this. The ultimate destination for a pilgrimage was the Holy Land. But there were other destinations in France, Spain and Italy. People wanted to make a pilgrimage at least once in a lifetime. Many such people had never been outside their own neighborhood, so the pilgrimage was a real adventure. They would join up with people from all over Europe, people the like of which they would never encounter in their own village. The pilgrimage was the most interesting thing that happened in their lifetime. Meeting the people, talking with them was far more important and beneficial than visiting the shrine. The pilgrimage was an allegory for life. Chaucer forever immortalized the pilgrimage in his "Canterbury Tales."

When, we think of the journey of life, the going is more important than the arriving. We are not here to arrive somewhere. We are here to live, and to share our lives with each other. The whole meaning is in the going, not in the arriving. Our lives are the ultimate pilgrimage.

LET US TALK ABOUT MURMURING. Murmuring gets to be a fine art in the lives of some people. It is natural, but left uncontrolled, it can be a very destructive process.

When Moses led the Jewish people out of Egypt, they ended up wandering in the desert. The Book of Exodus relates that some of the people sat in front of their tents and "murmured." The problem with this process is that they did not "murmur" to Moses. Murmuring is always a triangular process. We murmur to a third party hoping the word will get back to the one we are mad at. Murmuring is not very honest, not notably courageous.

We murmur because we have suffered some kind of loss. We are hurt, depressed or angry. We are grieving. However, murmuring is a way to make our depression permanent, to make our grieving chronic. It can be a very destructive process. We must find a way to recognize our losses and confront our problem. We must find a way to move beyond hurts. To sit in front of our tent and "murmur" is not the way.

Murmuring hurts, chronic depression is a poison. Remember the grouchy woman in the movie "Steel Magnolias." She said, "I am not neurotic. I have just been in a bad mood for 40 years." She was a "murmurer!" It is not the way to go.

It has been said that resentment is swallowing poison, and then waiting for the other person to die. It is not the way to go.

D O YOU NOTICE how men are more than anxious to tell you about their thoughts while women cannot wait to share their feelings? Their ideas are in line with the book, "Men are From Mars, Women are From Venus." I must admit I have not read this book, but I must. Since I am (incurably) male, I usually call the book, "Men are from Mars, Women are From I Do Not Know Where."

As a male, it pains me to say it, but we must get better at this "feeling" business. The fact is that we, whether male or female, spend 90% of our time in our feelings, not in our thoughts. We like to browse in our thoughts, because they are so much more controllable, while feelings have a life of their own. For example, I cannot tell you when was the last time I had a peevish thought about existentialism. I have not lost sleep over existentialism in eons. But, the guy who last week inferred in the coffee shop that I was too short and too bald has got me in a vice.

Ideas might just change the world, but feelings rule our lives. We need to get in control of our feelings. We handle our feelings by talking about them. We really handle them when we can laugh about them. Mark Twain once said that in a truly civilized society, one would be allowed to shoot 3 people in a lifetime. That statement helped me see the absurdity of my anger more than any thought I ever had.

So, my brothers, welcome to the world of feeling. When your wife asks you what you think, always start your answer with, "I feel that…!" It will drive her crazy. She will wonder who you really are.

W E WERE ALL RAISED with the ideal of the so-called self-made man. We have expressions like, "pulling yourself up by your boot straps" and "God helps those who help themselves." We dream of being independent and in control. I have heard irreligious people say, "Religion is for those too weak to be in control." The general idea is, "Blessed are those who do not need God." The real beatitude says just the opposite.

There is a proverb: "The final power is to be at ease with powerlessness." We need to be real, in touch with reality. God is the only being with real power. The rest of us may have some power, but we are dependent upon God for most of what we are about. We need to be comfortable with our lack of power. There is so much that we have no control over. We can all think of something that could happen which would be so hard for us. Everyone says that God does not give us more than we can handle. However, I would not like that saying tried on me.

As children of God, we must live realizing that we are dependent on God. We trust that God will pull us through. If we are real, we learn to be comfortable depending on God. In time, we become at ease with our powerlessness. Really, this is just another way of letting God be God. We become happy when we realize that we are not in charge and do not have to be. There is much happiness to be found in following the slogan, "Let go, and let God."

W HEN SOMEONE tells you, "It's the principle of the matter and not the money," it is usually the money. "It's the principle." You hear this sort of thing in divorce actions and in almost every other kind of lawsuit. However, we do not need to go to court to get into self-deception. We human beings seem to have a capacity to make ourselves believe whatever we want to believe. In my past, some of my self-evaluations would have made "Star Wars" appear unimaginative. Especially when we consider our motivations; we tend to always get on the side of the angels. Our motives are pure! I am not so sure about those other folks!

All the spiritual experts of our tradition agree that honesty is an essential quality for spiritual growth. We must have a real understanding of ourselves to grow into God. God sees us as we are. We must be just as real. This is the same for any close friendship. In friendship, we give ourselves to another, but it has to be our real selves. For any relationship, including one with God, self-delusion is deadly.

The poet, Robert Byrne once wrote:

"O What a gift of God to give us,
To see ourselves as others see us."

This gift of self-honesty is a hard gift to receive. You always pay a price for honesty. We pay with our pride. And I think that most of us would let go of our money sooner than our pride.

If we are going to grow in the Lord, we must be willing to pay the price; we must be glad to pay the price. Intimacy with God is worth more than our false self.

THERE ARE SO MANY in our society who are in patterns of self-defeating behavior. Addiction is always self-defeating. A guy pours half a quart of liquid depressant (called Bourbon) down his throat every day and then says, "Why am I always depressed?" Selfishness is self-defeating. In life, we need people more than anything else, and selfishness drives people away. The fact is that in life, takers lose eventually and givers win.

Age gives us all a perspective on human behavior. When you are 50 or 60, you have seen the truth of the slogan, "What goes around comes around." You have seen the wisdom of the scripture quotation, "As you sow, so shall you reap." We need to build a solid life. We need to make our actions toward others so good that we would be glad to have them come back at us. We need to sow richly in our friendships so that we may reap richly in our loved ones.

Beware of self-defeating behavior. It exists in all of us. We are all inclined, at least at times, to act against our own best interest. Why do we do it? I do not know. I think the inclination is there. I think it is called "Original Sin." I do know that if you get up every morning and shoot yourself in the foot, life gets very painful. There are very few willing to sympathize with one who inflicts pain on himself. So, beware of self-defeating behavior. It is not a rare trait. Most of us are somewhat self-defeating.

Life is painful enough without doing yourself in.

"THE SECRET OF BEING miserable is to have the leisure to bother about whether you are happy or not."
-George Bernard Shaw

George Bernard Shaw did have a way about him. All we need to do to be miserable is to worry about ourselves too much. Selfishness breeds misery. For example, in 1977 I had a heart attack. Afterward, I felt small pains around the heart. I told my doctor and he laughed. My doctor was wonderful. He was not long on tact but he was huge on honesty. He said, "I have been inside your heart (called a heart catherization). You are not in pain. I will tell you when you have pain. Get on with life."

In my experience, this usually happens when we get sick. Sickness makes us very aware of ourselves. Sickness is bad for us (a fairly safe statement), not just physically, but emotionally and spiritually. Being sick makes us start each day by asking, "How do I feel today?" Nothing can make us unhappy quicker that this kind of self-obsession.

What George Bernard Shaw said is just another way of saying what Jesus said. Whoever wishes to save his life will lose it. The one who is willing to let go of his life will save it. Jesus and His wonderful playwright are both telling us that our personal happiness is a by-product of life. If we go after happiness as a goal, we lose. If we worry about the happiness and welfare of others, we find happiness ourselves

So many people have a talent for misery. Jesus saved us from being one of them.

"I HAVE SEEN A THOUSAND tragedies in my life and most of them never happened."

   -Mark Twain

   It is not the real disasters in life that make us unhappy. It is the ones we make up in our own mind. After all, unless one is terribly unlucky, real live disasters rarely happen. We can think up half a dozen to worry about every day. The reality is our mind is more poisonous than the reality in the world.

   Time is a mental construction of ours. The past no longer exists and the future does not exist at all. For us, the only time that exists is now. Yet, we can spend an enormous amount of our time worrying and fretting about the future. We thus keep ourselves in an unreal world.

   Living in the "now" is the only way to stay in what is real. It has been said that spirituality is an effort to cling to the "real." Living in the "now," living one day at a time, one minute at a time is a mental discipline that does not come natural to most of us. It takes a conscious effort to remain in the present. However, the rewards are abundant. One who lives only in the present need only take on the real disasters of the world, not the innumerable disasters of the mind. Most of the things we worry about do not happen. If we stay in the present, those things will not worry us.

URING THIS NEXT WEEK, we celebrate the Feast of Ash Wednesday, the beginning of Lent. It is a time to think.

On Ash Wednesday, the priest puts ashes on your head and says, "Remember that you are dust and unto dust you shall return." There are different ways of interpreting this simple statement. A morbid way: Remember that you are going to die and decay! Burr! A hopeful way: Remember that there is more to life that what you have here. Not bad! A cautionary way: Remember to not get too at home here, because this world is not permanent. As a warning, our statement is a treasure. It contains wisdom.

Christ lived in a society where most people were very poor. Yet, He warned them against materialism. By comparison, we today are rich beyond the imagination of ancient people. In the last week, I have eaten bread from France, pasta from Italy, oyster sauce from China, fish from Australia and cooked with wine from Germany. And none of this was very expensive. If Christ were speaking today, He would talk much louder and much longer about the danger of materialism.

The warning could also say, "Remember, do not depend on material things for your happiness, because they will never satisfy." We have all experienced the truth in this statement. People my age are usually much richer than in years past when we were growing up, yet I do not think we are happier because of this. We take for granted what we have and keep desiring more to be happier. This can go on and on. It never works.

So, take heed: "Remember that you are dust and unto dust you shall return." Think of Lent. Think of renunciation. There is only one way to discover if we really need something. That is, give it up.

LENT COULD BE a time of significant spiritual growth, for each of us. We have been asked traditionally in Lent to give up things that we enjoy. This is not to see how miserable we can become. This process of giving up is part of the journey of self-discovery. It is a very "Franciscan" idea. The idea is that we do not know who we are until we know what we can do without.

Many people describe our development as persons as a process of peeling away our false self until we get down to the real self. Who is the real me, the real you? A very wise man once said that the false self is the part of me that needs to be supported from outside myself, from the praise of others. The real self is that part of me that can be supported from within myself. All the "things" in my life are on the outside. The more I give up these "things" the more I will uncover the real self; the more I will discover who I am. I do not know who I really am, until I know what I can do without.

We live in such a prosperous world. We surround ourselves with luxury. I have gone through stores and suddenly realized that of the millions of dollars of merchandise here, there is nothing that anyone in the world really needs. We must distinguish "needs" from "wants." Lent can help us with that.

So can a trip to the Third World. In Central America, I learned that I did not really need hot water, air conditioning, or a garbage disposal. I like those things, but I can do without them happily. If I give up the garbage disposal, do I get closer to God? No, that is ridiculous. But every time I use that appliance, I remember that I do not really need it. That way, I get closer to who I really am.

So, I recommend some "giving up," some abstinence. The "real self" is waiting. Happy Lent!

THE SEASON OF LENT is upon us. What are we going to do with it? I would suggest both a negative and a positive approach. As a negative approach, you could give up something. This is the old fashion Lenten penance, to give up some pleasure. We all gave up candy as kids, and then counted the days until Holy Saturday at noon. There is still great merit in this approach. We need to remind ourselves that we cannot be children of God and still satisfy every whim or desire. We have to be able to say "no" to ourselves. We cannot be children of God without being good at letting go. So, I suggest, pick one thing that you enjoy and lay off for 40 days.

Next, I think we need to do something positive during Lent. God is inviting us to intimacy with Himself. No matter how much we have responded to his invitation, we are not home yet. What could we change in our lives that would make us more available to God? This is a very personal question, but examples abound. We could entertain ourselves less (fewer movies, less TV) and spend that time in quiet with God. We could serve God's people more generously. There are people in rest homes that we are always going to visit.

Lent is a good time to remember good resolutions. We can give God time, by extra prayer in the morning, by a visit to church on the way to or from work, by turning off the radio and saying the rosary. Daily Mass or Mass once or twice a week extra is a great Lenten practice.

So, make a choice for Lent. Do not let Lent be just another period of the year. We can deepen our life during this time.

T HIS WEEK, we begin the sacred time of the church's liturgical year. It seems to me that the season of Lent and the celebration of Easter fall at the perfect time of year in the Northern Hemisphere. Our penitential season comes at a dismal time of year. Then Easter and spring arrive together. The feast of New Life comes with the season of new life. It all seems fitting. Since the Catholic church is a worldwide organization, the timing has to be accidental. I wonder how people in Australia celebrate Easter, coming right at the beginning of winter.

For us, as we go through the last month of winter, the church asks us to enter into the Lenten spirit, a time of mortification and sacrifice, a time of drawing into ourselves. Dragging through winter, we are in that kind of a mood already. Inside we are preparing for the celebration of the Resurrection. Outside, all nature is dormant waiting to come back to life. With any luck, the two big events will come together and we can celebrate new life both inside and outside.

The church asks us to imitate nature and make sure that we are giving birth to new life at Easter time. Spring should be on the inside as well as on the outside. The blossoming can be internal as well as external. No matter how old we are, there is still new life in all of us. If we enter into Lent in a generous spirit, we can find new life bursting out all around us and bursting out within us. Spring is a great time of year, a great time to celebrate Easter.

THE CHURCH DESIGNED LENT to be a time of special effort at our spirituality. It is a time to consider where we are and where we are going. None of us stand still in our spiritual journey. We are drawing closer to God or getting further away. There is no neutral territory. During Lent, we can take the time and make the effort to examine where we are with God. And to think about where we want to be.

Lent was meant to be our own personal private retreat. We only do what we want to do. No one is telling us how we must use the season of Lent. We have so many options. Extra prayer every day, scripture reading, other spiritual reading, fasting, visiting a relative in a convalescent home, writing a letter to a lonely relative, a special visit to church each week, Stations of the Cross, an extra Mass each week. The list could be endless.

Families could have a special scripture reading and prayer instead of grace before meals one time a week. Families could participate in Rice Bowl. When we do such spiritual exercises together with others, everyone benefits.

I hope you make this Lent your personal retreat. When the feast of New Life arrives, I hope we all feel more fully alive.

I N MY RECENT workshop in San Antonio, Texas, one of the speakers spoke of our passages in life. He quoted one of the great psychologists, saying that there are four births in a lifetime: natural birth, leaving home, late maturity and death. The first and the fourth are going to happen without any cooperation on our part. Of course, we can enter into the process of our own death. The second and third births need not happen at all, unless we make them happen. We only develop in life if we choose to develop. At every level, maturity demands an effort on our part. It does not just happen.

This kind of thinking stirs up some ideas within me. It seems to me that our religion, especially during Lent, is trying to tell us that we can experience birth or rebirth any time we choose. Every time we experience God in a new way, we enter a completely new world of spirituality. Every time, we are reborn. When the three Apostles went up on the mountain and saw Christ in all His glory, they had a new birth. When they came down from the mountain, their spiritual life was new, reborn.

This new experience of God is not something that happens every day. I would hope it happens not infrequently. It might happen as a result of our own effort during Lent. We might experience God differently at the birth of a child, or when a child first leaves home. This experience might come right out of the blue. However it happens, a new experience of God is always life giving, like birth. This is a good thought to keep in mind during Lent.

The Good News is: It is never too late to be born.

THE BEST THINGS IN LIFE are not things. We live in a world where we are deluged with voices that try to convince us that the above statement is not really true. All advertising is bent on that objective. Smart people pay a million dollars for 30 seconds during the Super Bowl. They think it works and I suspect they are right. I suspect that our economy would take a serious hit if we became convinced of the above statement.

This seems to mean that our way of life is based on a falsehood. Things do not bring happiness. We can keep that hope of material happiness alive. When we get more and more and do not achieve happiness, we say, "Let's try harder." So, we get more stuff. It goes on and on.

Christ gives us a different view of life. He thinks the best things in life are not things; they are people. They are relationships with people. Jesus thinks that the whole secret of happiness is loving others. Our happiness will be measured by the richness of our human and divine relationships.

What will make us happy is our capacity to give ourselves in love in the service of God and other people. This is the fullness of life. This is also a good thought to ponder during the season of Lent.

W E RECENTLY HEARD of the death of the singer Peggy Lee. You have to be a male of about my age to be interested in Peggy Lee. We of that generation remember best one of her songs, "Is that all there is?" This question was often asked by middle-aged men sitting in a bar. It was a haunting song. It is a haunting question.

You do not have to be an old guy sitting in a bar to stumble across this question. It is the most basic human question. Sooner or later, unless we are brain dead, we come to that question. "Is that all there is?" It seems that we are created with an infinite hunger inside us, and then we are placed in a world with very limited possibilities. Our lives must lead to this question.

The Spanish mystic, St. John of the Cross, calls this question the experience of "nada," nothingness. It is a profoundly spiritual experience. The question leads us to God. Because our answer to the question has to be "no," there has to be more than this, and that leads us to God.

If we were perfectly happy with our material world, we would see no need for God. However, we are not material beings; we are much more. There is a piece of God in all of us; a spark of infinity. We get lost in a material world. It in no way can fill the bill. We end up with Peggy Lee's question.

Lent is a time to enter into ourselves and realize the nothingness we find there. Then we are asked to reach deeper and find that piece of God, which exists inside. When we do this, we answer the question, "No, this is not all there is." And we begin to discover who we really are.

MANY OF US grew up in the church and experienced church, as I did, in the 40's and 50's. And believe me, church is different now than it was then. But it was real authentic church then and it is real authentic church now. Of course, the essence of church is the same; only the incidentals are different. But it all adds up to quite a different experience of church.

And it was ever so. In history, church has been an outlaw society, as in Roman times; church has been central to society as in the High Middle Ages. At one time, the church existed for close to two years without a Pope. It was still real authentic church. In England, they once had church largely without priests; the same was true in Mexico. And that was real authentic church. Whenever and wherever God's people come together, there you find church, real and authentic. The circumstances may be very different. The problems and the opportunities may be very different, but church is still there.

My mother, as a child, attended Mass once a month because of the distance. This was in the days before cars. That one Sunday each month was a wonderful all-day experience. Later in life, my mother attended Mass every day and she found that enriching.

For so many, real church is what they grew up with, and any change in that, they see as a violation of church. However, the real tradition of church is constant change. We must get used to the different faces of church. For it seems to me, the experience of church may change more in the immediate future than in the past. But we can be optimistic. The many faces of church are all wonderful, if we try to make them so.

WHEN IN HONDURAS, I attended mass on Sunday evenings in the little Village of Flores. The Mass was a wondrous experience of Liturgy. It took a few weeks to figure out why it was so great. There were many positives about the Mass. The people were alive and attentive. The singing was animated, if not great. But there was something more; there was community.

A young family was standing near me against one wall of the crowded church. Their two older children disappeared with their friends; one to be an altar server, one to sing in the choir. That left Mom and Dad with a little girl less than two. She had recently learned to walk and wanted to do so. She struggled with her mother until she let her wander. I watched her to make sure she was all right, but her parents did not. They were unconcerned.

I realized that this whole church was family. This little girl could not get away from family. Probably half of the people there were blood relatives, but they all were family. Everyone in the church knew and loved this little girl.

I watched. She tripped over a kneeler and fell. A big guy picked her up, hugged her, and played with her. She enjoyed that, but soon wanted to wander. Twenty minutes later, she popped up in the front of church. An older woman picked her up and played with her. She loved it and then escaped again. By the end of Mass, she had made the full circuit of the church and arrived back with her parents, marching up very proud of herself.

In Flores, there is little privacy. Everyone knows everyone else. There is community. They worship as family. The difference was quickly apparent to us visitors. The people of Flores do not have cars, and often no running water. But they have a first-rate church community and first-rate Liturgy.

I reflect. We value our privacy in our country, no one more than me. But we pay a huge price for our privacy; the price of community. It shows in our Liturgy. It shows in theirs.

CERTAIN PHRASES from childhood stick with us for a
lifetime. Think what this one brings to your mind: "Go
directly to jail. Do not pass go. Do not collect $200.00."
Wow! Does that bring back a bunch!

I have a sentence, which brings so many pleasant feelings to my
consciousness: "Let us place ourselves in the presence of God." This
was the first thing I heard each day for ten years during my
seminary career. To begin morning meditation each day, a student
in the back of the chapel spoke that sentence in a loud voice. I
always thought it was the best possible way to begin a day. My
day still begins with this statement.

I would recommend this prayer/statement for constant use
during Holy Week. When we begin Palm Sunday Mass, "Let us
place ourselves in the presence of God." Let us be with Jesus in His
march of triumph into Jerusalem.

"Let us place ourselves in the presence of God" on Easter
Sunday as we look into the empty tomb. Every time we celebrate
Mass, we re-enact the Paschal Mystery, Jesus' saving death and
resurrection. We are there! Let us be there with all our
consciousness. We need to repeat the constant invitation, "Let us
place ourselves in the presence of God."

A S WE GREW UP, we were exposed to the mysteries of Christianity. We learned about Jesus and all that He did for us, all that He gave for us. We came to a decision under the influence of our parents, as to how we would respond to these Mysteries of God's love. We became "religious." We adopted certain religious practices as a response to God. Going to Mass each Sunday was usually part of that response. In time, it all became rather habitual, and we could easily forget what we were doing, what we were responding to. This is the danger in the practice of religion. We go through the motions.

Every once in awhile, God wants us to reconsider the level of our response to His love. If I am 61 and I am still working on the level of response that I came to when I was 12, then I have lost my way. I need conversion. We all need conversion. In the natural process of life, we should be getting more generous. When people marry, they find new and deeper demands on their generosity. When they have a baby, the generosity demand goes up like a rocket. If you are ordained a priest, the same process occurs. God is constantly calling us through the events of life, to give more and more of ourselves.

We are now entering Holy Week. We concentrate on the reality of the suffering Christ on the Cross. We look at Christ and reconsider the level of our response. What we look at should motivate us. During this Holy Week, let us look at the suffering Jesus, and renew our commitment to the service of others, our commitment to our own personal growth. We cannot let ourselves float through life. This week is a wake-up call.

ACH YEAR IN LENT, the church asks us to experience once again the suffering, death and resurrection of our Brother Jesus.

The important word is experience. We do remember the events of our salvation during Lent. But we do more than that. We experience those events, and each experience of the Lord's Crucifixion brings us deeper into that mystery. It is a mystery of love and the deeper we get into that mystery, the more we can appreciate that love.

Each year we embark upon this effort to deepen our religious life by identifying with Jesus in His suffering, death and glorification. We ask everyone to do something special during Lent. There are all sorts of options. Attending daily Mass is a fine Lenten practice. We have Stations of the Cross on Fridays. A marvelous Lenten resolution is to stop in church every day on the way to work or on the way home for five minutes of quiet time with the Lord. This would be a great way to deepen our experience of the sufferings of Christ. A long quiet walk each day could do the same thing.

The church has always encouraged some kind of mortification during Lent. It is time to give up something. We could all afford to eat less, and less richly. We could all limit our television without personal loss. Whatever we give up will be a reminder of what Jesus gave up.

Remember, Lent was meant to be an experience. Let us share the experience of Jesus' suffering and enter into His love. May we be ready for Holy Week and ready to celebrate the New Life of the feast of Easter.

D O YOU EVER feel like you are spinning your wheels? If so, Greek mythology has provided us with a patron saint. His name is Sisyphus. He was the King of Corinth. He got cute and figured out a way to cheat death and thereby angered the gods. For a punishment, Sisyphus had to roll a huge rock up a hill. He could not possibly reach the top in one day, so when he quit working to sleep, the rock rolled back to the bottom. So, he would start over the next morning, on and on through eternity. He is the patron saint of those who do futile tasks, of those who spin their wheels.

Sisyphus lived life without meaning. I think he can help us find meaning. Let us suppose poor old Sisyphus could make it to the top of that hill. Suppose he piled up those rocks and then built a church. Then his life would have meaning. Right? But in 100 years, the church would fall down and all the rocks roll to the bottom of the hill. Where is the meaning of Sisyphus' labors? When our meaning depends on buildings, meaning is only temporary.

I do not know about you, but I spin my wheels a lot. I have a liking for Sisyphus; I know the feeling. But Sisyphus offers us no hope. However, Jesus does. Ultimate meaning comes from something that lasts. Only persons last for all eternity. Ultimate meaning can only come from people, how we treat them. Jesus said the love that we have for people would last. Love gives our lives meaning. Our love helps create persons, and those persons will always exist. What we do really counts.

If you are building a garage, you may be spinning your wheels. If you are loving your kid, you may not be. Because of Christ, we are not living lives of futile tasks. We are not Sisyphus. However, we could spare a kind thought for the poor old boy.

I N OUR DIOCESE, ordained priests lead most parishes. A few parishes are led by lay people. All of our parishes have lay people exercising leadership. This will be a more important factor as time goes on.

There are all kinds of leadership in the church. In the 12th Century, there was a pastor in a small town in Italy. I have always thought that this priest was the most unfortunate priest in the history of the church. Every Sunday he had to celebrate Mass for, and preach to, a little man in the pew. The man's name was Francis. The small town was Assisi.

How would you like the job of preaching every Sunday to the church's greatest saint? How would you like to be his leader? There are two kinds of leadership: legal leadership and de facto leadership. Legal leadership happens by appointment of authority. It is necessary; it is important. A legal leader has a paper on the wall establishing his leadership. De facto leadership comes from the Holy Spirit. It is most important. When someone stands out for their wisdom, for their goodness, for their sanctity, they tend to become leaders. They are not leaders because of a paper on the wall, but because, when they look over their shoulder, they see a crowd following.

The priest of Assisi was the first type of leader; Francis was the second type. There are very few legal leaders in the church. There are innumerable de facto leaders. They are becoming increasingly important. We need such leaders more and more. We, as a church, need to recognize and appreciate their leadership. Wisdom and kindness attract a crowd. Sometimes, the legal leader needs to get out of the way of the de facto leader. Priests have inhibited saints.

I look at the future with confidence because I see that our church has many wonderful leaders, legal and de facto. We are ready for the future. I am happy that each Sunday I do not have to look at a St. Francis in the pews. If there is one out there, I am blissfully ignorant.

I RECENTLY ATTENDED a workshop for those in ministry to people. During the workshop, it occurred to me that this title implied that some, if not most people are not involved in ministry. I think that this is a fiction, a myth. We entertain the same myth about leadership. We tend to think that leadership is rare. It is not. It is difficult to think of anyone who does not exercise leadership in some phase of their life. Maybe good leadership is unusual; maybe great leadership is rare. But leadership is a part of life, everyone's life. And leadership is just another form of ministry.

We can think of ministry by dividing the human race. There are ministers and those who are the recipients of ministry. Everyone ministers to someone. We are called to serve.

Example: my friend Pete lived half of his life in a nursing home paralyzed with arthritis. He could not move. He could do nothing for himself. Pete was ministered to constantly. However, Pete was also a minister. He was a teacher. He taught me patience. He taught me kindness under extreme stress. Quite possibly, he taught me better than anyone ever has. Pete was a minister.

Example: Martha was the last child in a large family. She was severely handicapped. Martha was rather helpless physically and emotionally. She was ministered to on all sides. But Martha had one talent. She was a great lover. Her love was pure. She loved just for the sake of doing it. She knew no other way. She ministered to everyone who came near her.

Do some people minister and some do not? Let us bury that fiction. We all minister, because there are people around us who are needy. We all lead, because there are people around us who are watching us. We need to concentrate on serving well, on leading well.

I bear the title of minister. I enjoy realizing that I have so much company.

I REMEMBER GOING to a Chinese restaurant once and watching the waiter write our order using Chinese symbols. They were not just letters like in our alphabet. They were like hieroglyphics. The symbols were very complicated, or so it seemed to me. They were beautiful. The waiter wrote them so fast and easily I was amazed.

I have heard that there is one symbol in Chinese for danger; there is another for opportunity. If the two are combined, you have the word for crisis. What a marvelous way of expressing the real nature of crisis.

Of course, we do not like problems or crisis. We are inclined to say, "Why?" or "Why me?" Every problem is an opportunity to become smarter, to become more patient, to grow. Every crisis is a pain, but it is also an opportunity. The Chinese seem to know this so well that the idea became a basic element in their language.

The next time someone rains on your parade, do not see pain or danger. See opportunity. You might start seeing opportunity all over the place. Then you do not say, "Why me?" Then you say, "Why not me?"

I thank the Chinese for their wonderful food, often, and I thank them for their wonderful way with words.

I N THE EARLY 1970'S, I met a man who had retired at age 65 and began to build a boat in his back yard. Not an ark, a 40-foot oceangoing sailboat. He did it all by himself. Experts told him that he could not cast the lead keel in his back yard. But he did! He built his own forge. He did not have a background of working with his hands, so he was constantly pushing himself beyond what he had thought were his capabilities. And push he did. He learned carpentry. He learned to splice wire cable together. He learned to design and sew sails. He built a 40-foot oceangoing sailboat! It took him five years. Then he sailed the Pacific. His name was James.

What amazed me about my friend James was his vision and his patience. At a late age, he started a project that would take years. He never knew if he would live long enough to finish, or if he would remain healthy enough.

Every day, he accomplished only a small fraction of that project and then had another go at it the next. He had a vision and he exercised the patience to see it through.

I am of the temperament that what I begin in the morning, I want to finish by the evening. A five-year project may sound staggering. Yet, the most important things we do are long-term affairs. Raising a child is a 20-year project. In any day, we make only a small contribution to the whole.

A wise man once said, "In our lifetime we accomplish only a tiny fraction of the magnificent enterprise that is God's work." My friend James helped me understand long-term vision. He helped me understand the importance of doing today's work, trusting in the future. James, wherever you are, I thank you.

"**A** REAL CONVERSATION no one owns." This statement comes from Fr. David Tracy, reputed to be one of the best theologians of the United States. He was one year behind me at the Gregorian University. I had no idea way back then how smart he was. Had I known, I would have been more polite to him.

His statement strikes me. I have been in many dishonest conversations. Superiors often do this kind of thing, be they parents, teachers, or bishops. It goes something like this: They say, "We have a problem. Let's sit down and talk this over." What they really mean is, "Baby, you are not going to get out of this room alive, until you agree with me." This is not a real conversation. This is laying down the law. Very often, not a bad idea, but why lie about it and call it a conversation?

Of course, we all have "bottom lines." We must have. But we need to state them honestly. In a conversation, we should not pretend that we are collectively looking for an answer, when we already know the answer. This morning I heard a teenage girl propose to her mother that it was a fine idea not to go to school today. She went on and on. There was no conversation. Her mother simply looked at her as if she had just landed from Mars. We all have bottom lines.

We need to be honest about our conversations. We may be totally open to anything, or we may have a firm answer already, or we may be some place in between. We can be honest about where we are. With kids, I often say "no" to any question, but then say that I will listen and maybe change my mind. I find that I can negotiate better from a "no" than from a "yes."

Let us always be honest. A real conversation no one owns.

I WAS RAISED IN a critical family. We were critical of ourselves first, but we did seem to have enough energy left to be critical of others. We were critical of politicians, our country, our church, our priests, and our teachers. We tried to be kind, but we did tend to be negative. We were also bright and perceptive. We saw that some things needed criticism. We saw that criticism could be a form of love.

I became accustomed to critical people. I have always liked critical people. I still do. However, somewhere along the line, I had to change. Criticism can be a form of love; it can also be a form of hatred. It can be a form of anger. There is a fine line between being a critic and being a cynic. Cynics in ancient Greece were those who did not believe in anything. The word cynic meant "dog."

There may be good reason to be critical. There may be reason to be cynical, but nothing positive ever comes out of it. Cynicism is a form of despair. It never corrects the situation. I found that I could not be around cynical people. There was just too much negativity.

There is an old slogan that says, "Live in the solution, not in the problem." Being in the solution is a way to make a critical nature into a virtue. To see a problem and go after a real solution is not negative or cynical. It is not despair. It depresses no one.

We need critical people. I hope I can walk the fine line between the critic and the cynic. I hope we all can.

WHEN A MAN with money meets a man with experience, the man with the experience ends up with the money, and the man with the money ends up with the experience.

I lived in Europe for four years and I traveled to all those different countries. It became clear to me that anyone in a strange country is vulnerable...a target. I knew that it was only a matter of time until I met someone who would trade some of their experience for some of my money. If I was not willing to accept this fact of life on the road, I should not travel. I should just stay home. In Naples, Italy, there are three dudes on every street corner willing to trade experience for money. They wait for any American tourist.

On a deeper level, we cannot become wise without experience, and experience always costs. We pay for most of our experiences not in money, but in emotional, if not physical, pain. Experience leading to wisdom never comes cheap. We have to make sure that the price is not too high. We have to make sure we learn from the experience. Otherwise, we pay twice. How many people do we know who married virtually the same person twice?

Life is too painful to pay for our wisdom more than once. When the experience comes, it is a gift, an opportunity. We must learn from our experience. Because we do pay the tuition price.

A CATHOLIC CUSTOM we have during Lent is the prayer we call the Way of the Cross. It is strictly Catholic. Some Protestant churches look so much like Catholic churches that people look for the Stations of the Cross to make sure they are in a Catholic church. We have developed this custom of prayer as a remembrance of the early Christian custom of walking the route that Jesus walked on the way to Calvary. This street later came to be called the "Via Dolorosa," the street of sorrows. We mentally make that walk in the Way of the Cross.

The Way of the Cross is a marvelous method of remembering the suffering of Christ. The Liturgy of Holy Week tries to help us do the same thing. We can put ourselves in the place of Simon of Cyrene, and walk through his last week with Jesus. We walk with Jesus into Jerusalem in triumph on Palm Sunday. We remember the only joy He had during that week. We sit with Him at the Last Supper. We watch His love for His friends and His efforts to make them understand. We watch what fear and anxiety do to Him in the garden, when His sweat ran "like drops of blood." We see Him through a humiliating trial and imprisonment. We walk with Him toward Calvary; we fall with Him; we die with Him.

And then we rise with Him. The message of Christ does not end with death. Death is not the last word for Jesus. Resurrection and new life are the last words. Palm Sunday was a triumph for Jesus, but it was nothing compared to Easter and the Resurrection.

The church asks us to make this walk with Jesus during Holy Week. The best way to express our faith in Christ, and to enrich that faith, is to make this walk. We create the "Via Dolorosa" in our lives, and we stay close to our Brother during His horrible week.

YEARS AGO, when I was pastor of the student parish at Western Michigan University, a group of us had an unforgettable experience. It was Good Friday; we were praying the Stations of the Cross. Every Good Friday, a dear friend of mine leads the Stations at the student parish. He still does. On that occasion, we had a huge Cross laid across the altar steps. Instead of walking from station to station, we asked participants to come forward and together lift the big Cross in the air. It took at least six people.

The crowd was mostly college students except for one old man, John, a friend of mine. Only I knew that John was seriously ill and had been released from the hospital that morning.

As my friend led us through the Stations, the college students came up spontaneously to lift the big Cross. By the 14th Station, all had taken a turn lifting the Cross. No one came up immediately until, John, the old man, still wearing slippers, got up, limped across the sanctuary and bent over to pick up that huge Cross. We were all shocked; no one moved. My friend in the podium, who tends to tear up when a cloud goes over, had tears streaming down his cheeks. Then, the "boys" went into action. Twenty college men vaulted over the front row of chairs and helped the old man. When they laid down the Cross, they put their arms around John and walked him back to his seat.

There was not a dry eye in the house. What a way to remember Jesus carrying His Cross! I am very sure that no one present has forgotten that particular celebration of the Stations of the Cross. It was a "miracle moment."

By way of footnote, old John died the next morning, Holy Saturday. We celebrated his funeral on Easter Monday.

THROUGHOUT THE MIDDLE AGES, the church building was thought to be the place where earth met heaven. The church architecture, so elaborate, so beautiful, was meant to be a representation of the celestial kingdom, heaven right here among us. That is why we kept such a respectful silence in church. That is why we made the sign of the cross with holy water as we entered. We were going into another world. I think that all this is rather a neat idea.

If we were to think that way during Holy Week, what would we have? The church would then be the place where we encounter Christ in the Last Supper; where we see Him suffer a mental agony in the garden; where He dies and is buried. Most important of all, the church would be the place where we encounter the Christ who rises to life, to show us that life is stronger than death.

I would suggest that we all think about the church building in this old fashioned way. The Middle Ages was a time considered ignorant, but they did come up with some good ideas. I suggest we think about having an encounter with Jesus during the most important week of His life. That encounter would take place where earth meets heaven. For us, that place is St. Joseph Church.

I suggest we meet Christ on 23rd Street, walk with Him through His suffering and death, and experience those events first hand. Such a walk could make His suffering more real to us. Then we will be ready to celebrate the Resurrection.

"HE IS RISEN." Are you? The Resurrection does not just occur after death. It can happen whenever we decide to begin living the Resurrected life. The Resurrection is not just an event; it is also a teaching. Christ did not just rise, He revealed the Resurrection.

In the Resurrection, Christ began to live in a completely new way. His relationship with the Father changed. He began to live the Resurrected life. Christ reveals this as a possibility for all of us. The Resurrection happened to Him, and it can happen to us. It can happen whenever we decide.

When we realize our dependence on God, the Resurrection is happening. When we begin to find our joy is God, we begin to live the Resurrected life. That is what happens in eternity. We see God. He is our source of joy. We do not reach the fullness of the Resurrection until eternity, but the whole process starts right now, if we want it to. We can be tied to the things of earth, or to things of heaven. Eventually, we will depend on God for our joy. Why not now?

When we decide to find as much joy in God as we can, the Resurrection is occurring in our lives.

So, how is the Resurrection going in your life? It is never too late to have a good day. It is never too early to experience Resurrection.

A S WE CELEBRATE the feast of Easter, we must see that this is a celebration of life. We are talking about Resurrection, the coming back to life of Jesus Christ. Coming to life is always an occasion to celebrate. When a baby is born, we overflow with joy. The celebration comes naturally.

In the Resurrection, Jesus tried to reveal to us the possibilities of life. When Jesus rose, He was not the same as He was before. His life was not restored; His life was transformed. His Resurrected life was a glorified life. We do not understand the nature of the risen life of Jesus, but we know His risen life was not limited like His previous life. The Resurrection tells us that there is such a thing as fullness of life. It holds out the hope for us that at some time life will be complete.

For fullness of life, we must wait until we enter eternity. However, we receive fuller life from God all the time. We need to see that God is giving this gift. Every day is a part of the gift. We need to hold out for ourselves the hope that life can be fuller right now. We all know this to be true. We all know that our feelings could be deeper, that our relationships could be richer. We know that we could enter more fully into life. This is God's gift of life. It comes now, not just in eternity.

I see many people who seem to be satisfied with just a minimum of life. They are satisfied with what they have. They do not seem to believe that life can be full and complete. We need to listen to the messages of the Resurrection.

We can be reaching for fullness of life every day and celebrating the renewed life every day. We can reach deeper into ourselves in prayer. We can reach for richer intimacy with our loved ones. Then we can understand that life is always something to celebrate.

EASTER CARRIES the message of Christ to us. It sums up what Christ came to say to us. Easter is the feast of New Life. In Christ's Resurrection, we see the new life that Christ promised to His followers.

Christ had a most optimistic view of human beings. He thought that human beings could be perfect. He thought that human beings could act like God. Jesus saw that we could love, that we could forgive, just as God does. Human beings can live without hatred, without resentments. We can live without violence. The power to be like this is within us.

However, many other things are within us too. We are very naturally inclined to be angry and resentful. An inclination to violence runs deep within us. You look at any movie, any play or novel, and the solution to the plot is almost always violent or a threat of violence. In our present state, we may have the power within us to be loving like God, but it is not likely that we will use it. The pull to be less than what we are is very strong. We can do it, but the odds are against us.

Jesus did not care about odds. He saw what the human race could be. He certainly knew that the whole human race would not embrace their full potential any time soon. Jesus also saw what each human could be. If the human race is not going to achieve perfection any time soon that does not mean that any one individual cannot.

This is the vision Jesus had of us. The human race may wallow in self-interest, but individual persons still can be all that God wants. There have been many wars, but there also has been a Paul of Tarsus, an Augustine, a Francis of Assisi, and a Therese of Lisieux. Christ brings New Life in the Resurrection—for me, for you.

JESUS LEFT a message behind. His message was contained in His words, but even more so, in His actions. His primary action was rising from the dead. In His Resurrection, Jesus was not just proving His authenticity. He was doing that, but much more.

By rising from the dead, Jesus was not so much telling us about Himself, as He was telling us about ourselves, and our future. The message of the Resurrection is that life is not in short supply. When Jesus rose, He was telling us that we would also rise. Death will not be the last word for us. Each one of us will live forever with God.

We are told that self-preservation is the most basic of human instincts. Christ is asking us to rise above this instinct because there is no need for it. God promises us eternal life. We do not need to struggle to preserve our life. We can leave it up to God. If we believe the message of the Resurrection, our life is assured. We can let God worry about that.

This one event makes all the difference in the world to every human person. We become free to make all the sacrifices Christ spoke of. If life is not in short supply, we do not have to hoard it up. We can give up so much in life or even life itself in the service of others. We are free. We do not have to worry about how it will all end.

The Resurrection is God's way of giving assurance that we can all end up well. The Resurrection is God's pledge that each human history can have a happy ending, if we only give ourselves over to God. When Jesus taught through His action at the Resurrection, He was at His most eloquent.

THE THEME OF this time of year is joy and thanksgiving. We have just celebrated the beautiful feast of the Resurrection. Outside, the world is beginning to come alive. Everything is changing, inside and out.

There were ancient cultures that did not understand that the coming of spring is inevitable. The world of winter is so drab, so dead. It seemed likely to them that new life might never come back. They thought it all depended on a whim of the gods. So, they fervently prayed each spring that the world would come alive again. But they always had serious doubt.

That is not so hard for me to believe as I look out on the world I see right now. Everything is brown and gray. It does seem hard to believe that the world can turn green as quickly as I know it will. What potential there is in the ground, in every tree, in every tulip bulb. God's power is all around us, and it is a loving, benevolent power.

A modest thought: if God gave so much potential to trees and tulips, what about each of us? It would be strange if God gave so much to plants, and not as much to His dearest children. Every person has the potential to burst forth into new life in the spring, in the fall, or at any other time. We are not on a schedule, but the potential for newness of life is inside. God is always helping us to begin life anew.

It is the time of year for joy and thanksgiving.

WHEN WE THINK OF "NEW LIFE," we tend to think of a newborn baby. This is the most obvious example of new life. But new life comes in many forms and at many times.

Example: A couple, married for many years, has adultery enter their life. One of them is guilty, and it becomes known by the other. They go through agony, hurt, anger, doubt, fighting, threats, depression; all the above enters the picture. And then finally forgiveness. If they stay together, they find their marriage different. There may be less trust at first, but also less taking each other for granted. It is new life.

Example: A wife dies after 50 years of marriage. The husband has to make that painful adjustment and learn to live alone. He may suffer much, but he learns to know himself deeper than he ever did before. New life appears.

New life is coming to us constantly. We are always encountering experiences that offer us life in a renewed way. These experiences can rightly be called "rebirth" or "resurrection." God gives us this gift of life at birth, and then asks us to plunge deeper and deeper into life. God will keep giving us more life if we ready ourselves.

The secret to fullness of life is to make sure that every experience is life giving, every encounter is a resurrection; every occasion leads to a rebirth.

BASEBALL SEASON HAS COME. I read recently about someone speculating as to whether there would be baseball in heaven. I do not think that baseball teaches us anything about eternity; I think baseball teaches us much about human living.

Baseball offers a good analogy of life, a good image, a good way of understanding. It would take an incredible hitter to get a hit in baseball every third trip to the plate. Even the best of hitters fail two-thirds of the time. Hitters learn to be patient; they learn to accept failure as part of the game.

In real life, we have to learn much the same lesson. In real life, we fail. We fail a lot. It is part of "the game." We can fail and fail in our efforts in life, and still succeed. None of us bats a thousand. If we succeed a third of the time, we are doing well.

I think of the lessons of baseball in regard to religious education. It applies equally to parents trying to pass on values to children. When trying to teach religion and Christian values, we do not need to "win" all the time. Most of the time, the young people we face cannot, or do not, hear anything we say. But every once in awhile, we say it in such a way, the message is really heard. That one time can change a life. I sat through thousands of religion classes in high school. Most of them were boring and vague in my mind. But, I distinctly remember three classes. And those three made a difference.

Baseball teaches us that we can fail and fail and still succeed, if we keep swinging.

Parents come to me: "My son is a drunk! My daughter will not get a job. Where did I fail?" I can only give to them the wisdom of a great baseball player-philosopher. Yogi Berra said, "It ain't over till it's over."

I WAS COMPLAINING about a person who at the time was driving me to thoughts of mayhem, when a friend of mine said, "You know, Jim, there is no such thing as a one-dimension person." I found that remark to be striking. After a few days' thought, I found the remark profound. And very helpful!

When someone irritates me, I tend to see only the irritation. I do not know anything about this person except that they irritate me. Do they have a mother? Are they sick or well, smart or dull? I do not know. I reduce such a person to one dimension. I only know that they irritate me.

All people are multi-dimensional. They do have mothers. They have feelings. They worry about loved ones. At times, they hurt; they are angry, disappointed, joyous, hopeful, and fearful. In other words, people who irritate us are pretty much like the rest of us.

The trick is finding that common ground that we can appreciate. The common ground is always there, because truly, there is no such thing as a one-dimensional person.

My friend who taught me this lesson was a good friend. She told me the truth. Strangely enough, the person who was irritating me at that time also later became a good friend. He was not a one-dimension person. And neither am I. We managed to find common ground.

F OR MANY YEARS, we were privileged to have a magnificent teacher of philosophy at Nazareth College. His name was George McMorrow. He was my good friend. He would tell his students that if they only remembered one sentence from his class, it would be all worthwhile. The sentence came from Socrates, "The unreflected life is not worth the living."

Upon this wisdom saying depends the richness of our lives. Human persons have the capacity to be like God, but we have an animal side as well. We share so much with the animal world, except we can think. We can reflect upon ourselves and what we are about. This puts us far above the animals. If we fail to use this ability to reflect, we remain with the animals and never rise to God.

An old Italian proverb says, "Better to live one day as a lion than 100 years as a lamb." Unless, of course, you are a lamb! To live an unreflected life is fine if you are a bulldog. But if you are a human person, the unreflected life is not worth living. It is a crime; it is a waste. It is to degrade God's glorious creation.

God has been so generous with His human creatures. We need to be ambitious for ourselves. We need to reflect upon ourselves and our ability to be like God. We can live on that. To do less is not worth the effort. We need to reflect the wisdom of the world's first great philosopher, "The unreflected life is not worth the living."

WHO ARE YOU when no one is looking? That should be such an easy question, but I am afraid it is not. We get so used to impressing others. To survive, there are so many people we must impress. It gets to be a habit. When do we give ourselves permission just to be who we really are? Of course, we want to put our best foot forward, but when it becomes a way of life, it can become dishonest.

There are people who do not try to impress. They make a point of just being who they are. Unfortunately, they are so few in number that they stand out. My dear friend, Fr. Edwin Palmer, was one of those people. He seemed to have no pretense. He most enjoyed telling stories when he looked ridiculous. He laughed all the time, but mostly at himself. Who was he when no one was looking? Who are you?

Of course, there is always someone looking. God is looking. So, who are you when you are alone with God? God knows us anyway, so any pretense is ridiculous. We save our pretense for others. But who are we when they are not looking? It is so important that we know.

A modest wish: That we be the same whether anyone is looking or not. Then we would be "cooking." They call such folks real people.

ROUND THE YEAR 400 AD, Augustine, a bishop of North Africa, was preaching on Sunday in his cathedral. It was hot, so the windows were open. From down the street, the sound of hymn singing could be heard in the cathedral. The rival Christian church, the Donatists, had their church that close to the official Catholic Cathedral. The brilliant Augustine was interrupted in his homily.

The Donatists were a schismatic group that had recently split from the Christian community in Hippo. The Donatists thought that the official church was too lenient in welcoming back sinners. Donatists were purists. They thought they were a cut above.

Hearing the singing from the Donatists, Augustine stopped preaching in frustration and said, "What a scandal we must be to our pagan neighbors. Christians cannot even get along with each other." Augustine then pointed out the window, and said, "They are like big frogs in a swamp, croaking. We are the only true Christians."

What strikes me about this story is that it is still going on today. Christians are still competing with each other and claiming the exclusive right to be called Christians.

A humble proposition: That we abandon the sixteen hundred year tradition of claiming exclusivity. We would do well to look into our own hearts and see how much real Christianity we find there. If we look long enough, I suspect, we will find some common ground with our fellow Christians. Then our religion would pull us together instead of pushing us apart.

Sixteen hundred years is long enough.

A LIFE IS PROPERLY measured by the quality of an individual's personal relationships.

The last time my parents gathered all their children together was on their 50th anniversary. All their children and in-laws were present as well as 29 grandchildren. Of course, they were glowing. My father spoke especially to his grandchildren and said, "When you are old, you realize that in life only one thing is important. How many people did I love and how deeply did I love them?" I saw profound wisdom in that statement.

I have seen so many famous people die and the obituary account lists all their many achievements. Yet, their family members saw them as strangers. To do great deeds in life is not enough. We must be great people. We must use our capacity for intimacy. We must be open to close friendships. In a word, we must be good at "loving." Loving is the power we have which makes us most like God.

In the end, I think our lives will be measured on the quality of our human relationships. This is where we must put our energies and efforts. At the end of our lives, we will see clearly that everything else is piffle.

AGE IS IMPORTANT only if you are cheese or wine. We make a lot out of age. We also come up with many presumptions about age. We presume that older people are wise. I wish that were true but, I must say that I know some older people who are definitely ignorant. Wisdom is like gold. It is where you find it. You might just find it in some young. Age is not that big a deal, unless you are cheese.

St. Clare of Assisi, under the direction of her friend named Francis, started a completely new religious order for women. She started from scratch. She did not try to copy any other religious order. Clare had so many decisions to make about how her sisters would live together. Decisions were always reached by consensus with everyone contributing opinions and ideas. However, Clare always insisted on hearing from the youngest and least educated women in the community. Clare said, "God would more naturally work through them." Age does not matter unless you are wine.

Every age has its own joys. I would love to run a mile as I did at age 17. However, at 17, I did not have nearly the confidence I possess now. I do not want to go back. In general, I would say that, given good health, being older is better than being younger. In my opinion, I carry a lot more peace inside than I did when I was 17. Age is not so important unless you really want to run a hundred yards in 12 seconds.

WHEN I WAS GROWING UP, on long trips in the car, my parents would get us playing games. I remember some of the games as being rather wonderful. They were quizzes. We would name a friend or family member and ask, "What is his best character trait?" or "What is his greatest natural weakness?" This was a great way to think about brothers and sisters and to really appreciate them.

We would sometimes switch around the quiz and ask, "Who is the most honest person you know?" or "Who is the happiest person?" Questions like these got us thinking about people. With the question about honesty, we all learned more about my grandfather, my mother's father. My parents told us all about his younger years. The old man lived with us and we loved him, but we never really knew him until the quiz.

My grandfather was honest to the point of absurdity. He once promised a man $300.00 in a business deal, later to find the man was cheating him. When the time came, he paid the $300.00 anyway. My grandmother had a fit. Grandpa said, "Because he is a liar does not mean I should get into the habit."

He was not Catholic; he did not even like the Catholic church. When he married a Catholic, he promised to raise any children Catholic. When his children got old enough, he gave up his farm and moved into the city so that they could attend Catholic school. His wife explained that he had not promised that much, but he said that he had. And he delivered.

After this particular game, we children never looked at grandpa the same way. That old man had many faults. He was a handful for my mother to care for, as I remember. But we never had to worry about him breaking his word. My grandfather did not do that.

I RECENTLY SAW THE MOVIE, "Groundhog Day." It is a wonderful story about a man who is caught in a "time warp." He was stuck in the same day. He lived through Groundhog Day, February 2, and every day thereafter was a repetition of that day. Every day, the hero got up and repeated all the actions of that day. Every day the same thing, round and round. Nothing that he did really mattered, nothing changed. The hero, of course, experienced frustration.

What if that person was you? Or me? What if every day was just about the same and we went round and round? Nothing we did seemed to change the world around us. Could we stand it?

Are we sure that we are not there now? Talk to a mother, who washes dishes three times a day, and changes twelve diapers, and makes five beds. What has any one of us done in the last month that has truly made a change in the world around us? Or in the last six months? Or in the last year? If you check the front page of the newspaper, you are hard put to see where the world has changed. Maybe we are in that same time warp already. Maybe the pragmatic value of our actions is just an illusion. We do seem to go round and round.

I think that the meaninglessness of our actions is the illusion. The dishes that are washed, the diapers changed, the beds made, are all acts of loving service. And love is never useless. Love enables the giver and the receiver. Love changes things. We cannot always see the change, so we have an illusion of sameness. Being there for our loved ones, and others, is not meaningless or useless. Love changes things. Possibly, only God sees the change clearly. Down deep, we refuse to believe that we are "spinning our wheels."

WE WOULD LIKE to think that life is logical, fair, nice and neat. We try hard to make it that way. We want life to be controllable. We would hate to think we walk through life without any control at all. But every once in a while, something happens that brings us down to reality. A young person dies, a child gets sick, or a baby is born handicapped. Then where do we go? It becomes evident that there is nothing logical about our world, that it is not fair, and that we are most certainly not in control.

This is the way it is. I do not like it; you do not like it. So what? Adjust! We must accept reality as it comes to us. We must learn to live with the mess.

An old slogan says, "Never let the sun go down on your anger." That is great advice, if you can do it. The problem is that often you cannot. You do the next best thing — you deny. You say, "I am not angry," as your knuckles turn white clutching the table. The slogan is really saying that we do not have to live with the mess. The slogan is unreal. Not all conflict can be resolved in a neat 24-hour period. Resolution takes time; denial is quick.

We do have to live with the "mess." Our lives are not neat; neither are our families nor our church, nor our country. If I could find a better deal, I would take it in a minute. And we can learn to live with it. Even better, we can learn to enjoy living with it.

After all, life is only a mess in our eyes, not in God's eyes. He is in control. If we depend upon Him, we may not understand the "mess", but we need not be threatened by it.

On any morning, it is all right to say to God, "Today I could do with a little less of the mess. How about a break?"

I RECEIVED A LESSON about the Holy Eucharist after twelve years of priesthood. It came from a layman. He was the father of twelve children, the oldest seven of whom had left home. His youngest son, Robert, was mentally disabled. Robert became very frustrated with his limitations and he often acted out. Robert was a dear. He was not violent, but he sure was loud at times.

One evening, I was celebrating a Mass in this home. Most of the older children had come back home for the occasion. Robert was seated in front of the altar. With all of the excitement, he began to scream and yell. I was at the altar getting ready for Mass. The father came over to Robert and an older daughter approached and said, "Daddy, I can take Robert upstairs where he won't disturb people."

The father put his arm around his daughter and moved her over to the corner. I listened in. He said very gently, pointing to the altar, "Dear, what this is about is real life. Robert is part of real life and he stays here!" That young woman had the good sense to look at her father and say, "Yes, Daddy."

I wanted to cheer! That was the best lesson in the Eucharist I ever had. It was far better than anything I was taught in theology. From that time on, I have never felt good about "cry rooms."

The Holy Eucharist is about real life. No phase of real life is inappropriate for the Eucharist. Real life is messy. We all belong at the Eucharist. At our best, at our worst, we belong at the table of the Lord. At that table, we celebrate real life.

AS OUR SECOND graders receive their First Communion, I recommend that we all enter into their First Communion. Every year when I see these little ones come to Holy Communion so anxious, so prepared, it makes me consider how prepared I am to receive. I am sure I am not prepared as well as they are. We do get so accustomed to receiving Holy Communion, that it becomes routine. We can receive Communion over and over again without a thought of what we are doing. We can enter into their Communion, by doing better ourselves. We tell these children that God is entering into their lives in Holy Communion and that they must pay attention. God enters into all our lives constantly. Am I attentive to His presence? Are you? We can enter into their First Communion by sharing their attentiveness to God in their lives.

Let us share their joy. May we allow them to inspire us to a greater consciousness of God in our lives. Let us rejoice!

These little people are well prepared to receive Communion today. They have been preparing for months. I hope we are as well prepared to receive Communion today as they are. I hope we receive as consciously as they do.

ON SATURDAY, 58 of our second-graders received their First Holy Communion. This is a most important occasion in their lives. We all remember our First Communion day. It is one of the small number of events that stand out for everyone. For me, between my baptism and my ordination to the priesthood, there was one spiritual event of note, my First Communion.

One of the great spiritual giants of the Catholic tradition was the 13th Century Dominican Meister John Eckhart. One of his insights into spirituality is that God wants to be close to us far more than we want to be close to God. The real compelling desire is on God's part. Just think how this applies to our little second-graders. If God wants to be close to jaded older people like me and some of you, (and He does) just imagine how much He wants to be with our little ones. How could He not be overcome with longing?

The Lord's Supper is the central act of the Catholic community. Our children are the most precious part of our community. Of necessity, we have to leave them out of full participation in the Lord's Supper. Now their time has come. It will be such a pleasure for me to lay the Holy Eucharist in their hands, and not just pat them on the head. They are one with us now in the celebration of Mass.

So, we congratulate our little ones. We rejoice with you.

A T THE END OF THE 12th century in Italy, there lived a man who was possibly the most unique person who ever lived. He was, of course, Francis of Assisi. His father thought he was crazy. He was crazy, if you call crazy differing from normal thought patterns and normal patterns of behavior. Francis did differ. For real!

Francis of Assisi introduced us to what I call the "Spirituality of Subtraction." We think of becoming spiritual as adding things to our lives. Pray more, go to church more, attend more Masses, etc. This is the spiritual road. For Francis, spirituality meant removing things from our lives. The simpler we live, the more spiritual we are. For Francis, letting go was the key. Let go of possessions, let go of ego, let go of luxuries, let go of everything that is not God. Spirituality is not a process of adding. It is a process of subtraction.

In my opinion, no one ever subtracted as much as Francis did. We are certainly not going to be another Francis of Assisi. I am not so sure we could take another Francis. However, Francis has something to teach us. We all need to let go of something. I have never made a step forward without letting go of something. So, what do I need to let go of? What do you need to let go of? If we let go of some things, we would be happier; our loved ones would be happier.

Was Francis crazy? He certainly was abnormal. There is another word to describe his abnormality. The word is "sanctity."

YEARS AGO, I saw a striking movie "The Great Waldo Pepper." It was the story of two fliers. One, a German, had gained fame in World War I. Later, he came to the U.S., was famous and made a fortune in the movies. Then there was Waldo Pepper. An American, he was too young for WWI and gained no fame. He was as talented a flier as the other man, but he was a "day late and a dollar short" all his life. He flew at county fairs in the U.S. and no one ever heard of him. He was always broke.

Years later, the two fliers worked on a war movie together. They were to fly against each other. They recognized that they were kindred souls. They recognized something else in each other-despair. By unspoken agreement, they flew up and killed each other.

The movie was so striking. One man achieved all of his goals in life. He had everything. The other achieved nothing. Yet, in the end they were both in the same place emotionally, in total depression. Watch out for your values. Watch out for your goals. If you pick the wrong goals, it will not matter whether you get there or not. Money goals are not worth chasing.

We are free. We can choose the values in life that we desire. All of our happiness depends on making that choice wisely.

T S. ELIOT WROTE the wonderful play, "Murder in the Cathedral". It portrayed the murder of Thomas Becket, the Archbishop of Canterbury. Four knights did the deed. Afterwards on stage, they rationalized their action. One knight said, "We had to do it for the good of the country." Another knight, "We got nothing out of this. It was our duty." A third said, "Thomas provoked us. We did not murder him. He committed suicide."

The play reminds us of our capacity to rationalize anything. We can think up such pure motives for rather questionable deeds. While I was on the board of the shelter home for battered women, men would explain to me why they had to beat their wives. I knew a couple once that beat their children because the Bible told them to do so!

This kind of rationalization can lead to spiritual death. The worst thing we can do for ourselves is to declare our faults to be virtues. Then there can be no repentance and no change. No one turns away from "virtue."

We need to see ourselves as we are. A father cannot let go of his children and interfere with their adult lives. He says he is only being a good father. But good fathers let go at the appropriate time. We say we cannot tell a friend the truth about himself, because it would hurt his feelings. We love him too much. But good people tell the truth despite the consequences.

We cannot arrive at perfection if we declare we are already there. Rationalization puts us in a false world, a world of lies.

Let us be real.

SIXTEEN YEARS AGO I made a directed retreat at Monresa Retreat House in Detroit. As in all directed retreats, I was alone and the director was my Jesuit friend, Fr. Jack Shuett. I made notes of my reflections during the retreat. Recently, I found those notes. One page said, "The way I think about time, the way I use time is one of the most basic issues in my spiritual life." I do not remember writing that. However, I most certainly agree with that statement. If it was true then, it is still true.

I need, and we all need, to live the vast majority of our time in the present. We can easily spend great amounts of our time brooding about the past. We can latch on to every hurt we have ever experienced and live it again and again. With this approach, it is never too late to have a miserable day.

Another approach to the question of time is to worry about the future. Mark Twain once said, "I have had a thousand trials in my life, and most of them never happened." If we live in the future, we can be unhappy most of the time. There is no end of worries we can imagine in the future. Parents can, and do think of all the awful things that could happen to their children and are frantic.

If we are brooding about the past, or fearful about the future, we are missing the gifts God is giving us this day. We cannot be grateful unless we live in the present. Healthy spirituality is now, not in the past, not in the future. It is now. Spirituality means we must practice mental discipline to live our lives in the present, to live one day at a time.

"The way we use time is basic." Not a bad reflection for a 45-year-old!

I N THE 1960'S, there was a song with the famous line, "Freedom is just another word for nothing left to lose." This is a rather grim version of freedom. However, there probably is no other way to be sure that we are free of anything until we get along without that thing.

I went through an experience of freedom and the lack of freedom in 1973 during the gas shortage. I wanted to go to Detroit for a family affair, and since I was not sure of a gas supply in Detroit, I realized I could not go. That was the first time I had such a limitation since the gas rationing of World War II days. Cars give us so much freedom, yet when you cannot use them, you realize you are lost without them. Do cars offer me freedom or addiction? The same thing could be asked of so many things in our lives, including electricity, telephones, TV, and computers. Are they freeing or enslaving?

I do believe that the answer lies in how we use the things we have. How do we see those things? I would be crazy never to turn on a light just because some day the electricity might go off. We can use things without depending on them to the point of addiction. We can use things and still be detached, but it is a tricky affair. This trick amounts to how to be Christian in a prosperous world.

I see many attitudes I admire in Honduras. However, I do not want to adopt their poverty to acquire their virtues. Can I transplant their attitudes into my own world? I hope I can.

I believe that I must be ready to let go of anything at the appropriate time. And God says when that is. I must be willing to let go of anything except God. Ultimately, true freedom is still another word for nothing left to lose.

A TRUE STORY: Once upon a time, there was a public school in New York City, in Harlem. It was called PS 121. It was not a particularly good school. The majority of its students did not finish high school; they quit and became a problem for society. Less than 2 percent of its students went on to college. It was not a pretty picture.

Then the picture changed. A man who was a graduate of PS 121 came to talk to the students. He had been very successful in business, a millionaire. He stressed the importance of education in the future lives of the students. He told the students that to live a happy life, they needed to finish school.

Then he did more. He took the next step. He enabled the students by giving them a vision. This marvelously wise man pledged that any student listening to him at that moment, who finished high school, would have their way through college paid for out of his own estate. The man at that time set aside the huge amount of money it might take to keep that pledge.

On that day, PS 121 started to become a different school. The students began to see that they had a future. They began to work toward future goals. The dropout rate fell to less than 10 percent and about 80 percent of those students enrolled in college after high school. Over half of those finished college. The school became different because one man gave those students a vision, and he gave the support to make that vision a reality. But the students still had to do the work.

Not one of us can accomplish anything without a vision. We cannot do what we cannot imagine. When we can see the possibilities, then we can achieve. That man in Harlem gave those students a peek at the possible future. That vision made a difference.

I ONCE READ that there are Four Commandments of Contentment. Since I am never filled up on contentment, I was interested.

Commandment Number 1: "Thou shalt live in the here and now." There are so many worries in our future. If we live there, we will always be worried sick. We have made so many mistakes in our past. If we live there, we will be perpetually embarrassed or ashamed. The "here and now" is the only place to be happy.

Commandment Number 2: "Thou shalt not take thyself too seriously." I must remind myself that my middle name is not "Messiah." There is a Savior; He is simply not me. I am in control of very little in the world. I do not have to take so much responsibility. I can let God run the world.

Commandment Number 3: "Thou shalt not be in a hurry." The old adage, "Stop and smell the roses," is more important, more wise, the older I get. God surrounds us with beauty. We can waste it all by rushing.

Commandment Number 4: "Thou shalt be grateful." It is hard to imagine a truly grateful person being unhappy. This kind of gratitude is not a spontaneous emotion, but a resolution. We must be aware of our blessings; we must be grateful. This attitude leads to contentment.

Such are the Four Commandments of Contentment. Of course, we know that only relative happiness comes in this life. Ultimate, complete happiness is found only in eternity. We do not get the whole cake here. But part of the cake is wonderful. The Four Commandments lead us there.

Y OU HEAR A LOT OF TALK about "burnout" these days. This is a state when a person has so much stress in their life that they can no longer cope with their lives. They just cannot keep going. This may be very serious where they need psychological treatment and rest for a period of time. Or it may be a simple setback. They may need three martinis and a good night's sleep. Or they may need a solid half hour sitting in the presence of God in profound contact.

Slogan: Burnout happens not because of too much work, but because of too little intimacy.

Stress is different for every person. What would break my back might barely make a dent in another person. I have sat in kitchens where the children are making so much noise that it was bedlam. Mom is sitting with me carrying on a "normal" conversation. I am going crazy, and she does not even hear it. Stress is relative to the person. I have been in foundries and I do not think I could work there. The noise is too much. But men do work there and they cope. How do they cope? Maybe by going home and kicking the dog. Hopefully by going home and talking to their wives and replenishing their energies. Talking to a loved one, a spouse, a child, or God can make a person see that it is all worthwhile.

That is called coping. If you are up to your neck in stress, and up to your nose in coping ability, you are doing fine. Burnout does not happen from too much work, but from too little intimacy. We can do almost anything with a little help from our friends.

" THERE SHE LAY IN HER BED, still as I watch her sleeping. My thoughts turn to questions: Why God, cannot she speak? Why can't she think rational thoughts? Why is her mind so weak so that no meaningful cognition emerges from it? Her eyes are insensitive now, her muscles weak. She has no stamina and is now completely dependent upon her caregivers for everything. She cannot feed herself; she is incontinent of urine and bowel. No fine motor skills has she, no sense of taste. Indeed, all of her senses are dim now. She drools and she whines; tears occasionally roll down her cheeks. She seems generally unable to care for herself in any way. She appears helpless."

When we read the above paragraph, we wince. We perhaps remember older people we attended during their time of death. We may even be thinking of our own mother. Maybe it makes us think of Dr. K, and the very important controversy of our day. When life is over, why not end it? We think, "Isn't this too bad?"

Except this paragraph is not describing an old and feeble woman. It is a description of a two-week-old female infant. The reality is so very different, but the description still fits both the aged and the infant. We would never say, "Isn't this too bad?" about the infant.

The infant is brimming with life. In the eyes of God, so is the old woman. She is on the brink of eternal life. The older person is closer to the fullness of life than the infant is. We can see old age as God sees it.

OUR FAITH IS a way of being held by God. God always holds us in love, in affection. That is the Good News. God's "holding" never changes. We can count on this affectionate Father.

How does the Catholic church hold us? The church used to hold her people in a paternalistic manner. The church was our Mother guiding us children through life. The problem was that the children never grew up. The church needed to be populated with adults, not children. The church, like other parents, needed to find a way to hold its members like adults. The church is "us," so we are really talking about how we hold each other. How do bishops and priests hold lay people and vice-versa? The parent-child model will not serve. We must hold each other in respect, in accountability, and always in love.

How does the church hold us? In a parental embrace? That has been changing for some time. It means our idea of authority changes, too. It is not an easy change. It is not easy to stop loving like a parent. Ask any parent whose child just went off to college. This change of our embrace with the church affects all of us. As a priest, I need to hold others in accountability; others need to hold me in accountability. We must always hold each other in respect. To be like God, we must hold each other in love.

WHETHER YOU LOOK at the prophets of the Old Testement or our modern prophets like Mahatma Ghandi or Martin Luther King, we find that prophets tend to be lonely, singular people. They have an insight, an awareness of reality that others do not share. They are driven to reveal their awareness, which is usually unpopular. They commonly are not very emotionally well-rounded people, because their awareness makes them so alone. They need friends, but they find that no one really understands them. Remember Christ in the garden before His death.

Sometimes prophets had friends. Even though the friends did not fully understand, they could still be supportive of the prophet. For example, the apostle John was such a friend for Jesus. When the other apostles ran away in fright, John stayed close to Jesus, even on the cross. John did not really understand why Jesus was doing this, but he was not going to let him do it alone. John was known among the apostles as the disciple that Jesus loved.

Each of us probably will never know a real prophet, but we do know people who tell the truth in our world and are therefore not overly popular. They may not be Major Prophets, but they are prophets with a small "p," and like Major Prophets, they need support. We must love truth when we find it, and we must support the messenger of truth. We need all the prophets that God sends us.

"EVERYTHING CAN BE done better." This statement can drive us all crazy; crazy with guilt. A friend of mine was a writer for a newspaper. Such people must live with deadlines. My friend was obsessed with perfection. He was always late, to the point that he was almost fired. His boss would scream "Enough! Good is good enough!"

When is good, good enough? I would say, "Today." We just have to settle for the "good" today. The "perfect" will come later. We are called upon to strive for perfection, but we are not expected to achieve perfection immediately. It is a lifelong quest. One of the founders of Alcoholics Anonymous poked fun at the guy who wanted to get well "by Thursday." He knew that recovery is a lifetime project. We will mess it up if we are in a hurry.

Sooner or later, we must say to ourselves that it is OK for me to be me today. It is OK for me to be me with all of my imperfections. I must be on the way to perfection, but it is OK today if I have not arrived at perfection.

To be a good enough father/mother today is good enough. You can go to bed and sleep well. To be a good enough priest today is good enough. That attitude does not mean that we are not striving for perfection. It just seems that we know we are on a long journey to perfection. We can enjoy the journey. We do not have to feel bad about ourselves every night because we are not at our destination yet.

So go to bed and say, "It was a good day. Not perfect, but good enough. I can rest now." Everything can be done better. True! But it need not be done better today. Let's give ourselves a break and relax. Good is good enough.

LIKE SO MANY people on planet earth, I have, once upon a time, gone to Walt Disney World in Florida. As everyone else, I found the place to be wondrous. However, it was different from what I expected. I did not enjoy Disney World. I enjoyed the kids enjoying Disney World. To experience the wonder of life through the eyes of a child is the greatest.

My first experience of this was with my nephew, Daniel. He was about seven when a neighbor at their house on a lake stopped to ask if wanted a ride in an all-terrain vehicle. It could go on land, over water, anywhere. When Daniel returned, he was not high; he was in orbit. I have never seen a face so radiant with excitement. I did not need the ride. Seeing Daniel on the ride was all the excitement I needed.

What I saw at Disney World was the look on Daniel's face multiplied by 500. After all, I am an adult. I do not want to hug Mickey Mouse. But, man, is it great to watch a child hugging Mickey Mouse. And at Disney World, there is magic everywhere you turn.

Children do not need to go to Disney World to find magic. They can find magic in a leaf or in a dandelion. If we are on the ball, we can watch that face as they see magic. We must remember: To experience the wonder of life through the eyes of a child is one of life's great gifts.

I REMEMBER CELEBRATING a wedding. I was standing up front watching my friend Jim walk his daughter down the aisle. Jim was a mechanic. He had great hands, calloused and grease embedded; not like the "sissy" hands of his pastor! Here he was, approaching me in a tuxedo with his daughter in a glorious white dress, a dress she would never wear again.

I remember thinking of how unreal all this was. Everything seemed abnormal and inappropriate. Years later, I read a book on anthropology by Victor Turner, "On the Edge of the Bush." This scholar explained that these special clothes have a meaning, going back to the ancient history of man.

In times of transition, people wore strange clothes that they never wore at other times. It signified that they were in a time of transition, an "in-between" state. The bride in the white dress is no longer her father's daughter, but she is not yet her husband's wife. She is "in-between."

It makes sense. Transition times are so important. How we adjust at transition times determines how we will live. The special clothes stress the importance of such times. It makes sense.

I stand at the altar in special clothes. I would not wear those clothes in any other place. I am not just Jim O'Leary there. I am a priest. I am "in-between" now. I stand between the people and God. I represent God to the people, and the people to God.

Transition times are most important for us. God works through transition. We often wear special clothes to remind us of its importance, just like our ancient ancestors. It makes sense.

MUCH OF OUR success in life depends on how well we handle transition periods in our life. I think of that at this time of year, because so many around me are going through transitions. Our fifth graders move on to middle school, our eighth graders to high school, and our graduates move on to college or that place called the "real world."

These are all important transitions in life. All of our children must get used to a new level of maturity. They must respond to a new level of maturity. Each new phase of life brings bigger responsibilities. If we do not respond well at each phase, we will never be comfortable in life. I certainly know adults who still belong in high school.

These transitions are certainly not the biggest transitions in life. They get us in practice for the huge transitions of marriage or the pain of losing a loved one in death. When each phase of life begins, it is so important to start well, to make the adjustments and get on with the work of life.

I do not think that it is possible for children to know how much they are loved throughout their life. Those of us who have not had children cannot really understand the feeling of a parent holding their child for the first time. "You gotta be there." You gotta be a mother, a father.

Of course, after graduation the love does not end. But the relationship does go through a change. College students have more independence from Mom and Dad. That can lead to good things on both sides. Parents appreciate children more and vice versa. Leaving home is a nice way to realize how nice home was.

FRIENDSHIPS, especially between the sexes, can always have the underlying idea of how can this other person make me happy. To the extent that such an idea is present, the friendship is sick. Real love is always a reaching out to be concerned about and to serve the other person. The more we care about ourselves, the less friendship we share. Selfishness is not the basis for two people to come together. It is the basis for aloneness.

One of the harsh facts of life is that no one can make us happy. It is impossible. My happiness depends on my insides. My attitudes determine my happiness. My expectation in life, my level of anger, my capacity to forgive; these are the things that make me happy or miserable. No other person has control over them. A second painful fact of life is that no one wants the job of making me happy. No one was born for that task.

We must make ourselves happy. We are each born for that task. We have the equipment and the power. We can develop expectations and attitudes that lead to happiness. I can absolve others of the task of making me happy. In this way, I can make friendships based upon mutual caring and not based on my own need.

I do not need a friendship to make me happy. I can seek a friendship to share the happiness I have achieved within myself. Then, I am a friend. Let us remember that friendship is the richest word in the English language.

S PIRITUALITY IS about our personal relation with God, but religion is more than that. Spirituality is about God and me; religion is about me, God, and a whole bunch of other people.

I think it is the other people that present the problem. I want to put my energy into the celebration of Mass, but what if the priest is a drunk, or is quite unkind, or both? What if the lector stole my girlfriend when we were 16? Maybe then I would rather take a quiet walk in the woods and be alone with God.

That is not enough. Spirituality cannot be just between God and me because life cannot be just between God and me. There are people out there, and how I treat them influences how I relate to God. We do not need to join a religion to encounter those people, but we do find others in organized religion, and they do confront our spirituality.

The New Testament brings spirituality and religion together. Jesus said, in a vision to St. Paul, "I am Jesus whom you persecute." Where is God? You find Him in people. Whether we find people in church, at our job, or in the Kiwanis Club, how we treat those people determines what our spirituality will be like. No one goes to heaven alone; we bring each other along.

So, we can say with much truth, "Church would be great, except for those people." But the church is those people. And other people confront our spirituality and make us see how real our spirituality is. Other people keep us honest.

Christian spirituality is always about more than God and me. It always involves other people. That is where it gets messy.

"IF YOU CAN SEE the road ahead, it is not worth the trip." The great Italian poet, Dante, wrote the above words. They are worth a look.

We all have a need for security. We want to know where we are going. We also have a great desire for adventure. Surprises can be painful, but they are not boring. We crave excitement. Surprises cause us to react and change our course. That process can be creative and exciting. The great voyages of history were adventures. Columbus thought he was going to India. Many of the great discoveries of science and medicine were accidental.

Do we really always want to see the road ahead? Surprises can be more fun. That is fortunate, because life is not a sure thing! Life brings almost constant surprises. In life, we are almost always working on Plan B. Plan A works for almost no one. We are all on plan B, or C, or W. Real life never goes as planned. We must always be ready to adapt.

This might not be acceptable for those who have worked hard on their retirement plan. But we had better get real. God is ever changing and so is His gift of life. Real life is about Plan B, and real life is always creative.

A T THE BALLOON FESTIVAL, I saw a small child wander away from her family. Suddenly, she looked around and saw only strangers. The joy in her face turned to fear, then to panic. She screamed and started to cry. Her mother was there in a few seconds. Although she wandered away from Mom, Mom did not get far away from her. The lesson was learned. This little girl should not get too far away. She needs Mom. She is dependent.

We all admit our dependence upon God, but in our world, when & how do we experience that dependence? It seems to me that in our world everyone believes they depend upon God, but few people find that fact very real in their lives. Nothing is real until it happens. We have become prosperous enough to hold off all the unpleasant realities and thereby avoid the experience of our dependence upon God. We depend on our income, our insurance plan, our health care system, and our retirement preparations. We depend on ourselves. Disaster can strike, and does, but not too often and hopefully, not to us.

So how do we experience our dependence? When was the last time you had such an experience? It is not a frequent happening in our world. How can we bring this about? We really do not want to look for a way to get an exotic disease in order to experience our dependence. Can we find a way to experience who we are, to know who we are, and to know, truly, who God is? We would then know what our relationship is and that it is not a relation between equals.

I think ambitious prayer can give us that experience of who we are and Who God is. I say ambitious prayer because we must be trying to achieve something precious, something only God can give. Intimacy with God is that precious something. We cannot earn this or work for it. It is God's gift. We depend upon Him to give.

If we only want the minimum from life, we may make it alone. If we are ambitious, we will need to depend upon God. We need this experience. It is either get deep into prayer, or get lost at a balloon festival.

THERE ARE MANY ways to be a father. I recently got together with an old friend, a young man I taught in high school. We have met about once a year, for the past forty years. My friend married young and divorced after a few years and two children. He moved to Detroit and his children remained in Kalamazoo. Every other weekend he made the round trip to be with his children.

However, he did something else that I thought was quite special. He explained to his children, "I am going to call you on the telephone every night, just because I want to hear your voice." He explained that they could talk for an hour or for a minute, or not at all. If they were busy with a friend, they could just say, "Hi, Dad." That was acceptable. He just wanted to hear their voice every day.

Through their growing years, these two children heard from their father every night. My friend was an extraordinary father. Would it have been better if he had lived with his children? I would think the answer would be "yes." But that option was closed down, and he had to develop other options. And he did! There are many ways to be a father.

What is the essence of father? Playing catch with a son? A blind father has a problem with that. Putting the kids to bed each night? A truck driver father has a problem with that. The essence of father is to love, to care, to serve. There are many ways of doing that.

By the way, there are many ways of being a priest, mother, big sister, uncle, or even a good person. We all have to be creative. God calls each of us to excellence. We have to figure out how to get there. Happily, there are many ways.

"WERE NOT OUR hearts burning inside us as he spoke to us on the road?" Luke 24.

This burning heart business, how do we keep it going? I wonder about those two disciples. I wonder how long their hearts were burning over the message or the person of Jesus. I would be willing to bet the burning lasted a lifetime. But it was not the same as on the road to Emmaus. Nothing sustains that kind of enthusiasm permanently. But we do want to keep burning.

How long do married couples keep their burning going after the wedding? I hope the love goes on forever, but almost certainly, the passion will not. I must admit, after a wedding when I hear them singing, "Please Release Me" on the way out of church, it does give me an uneasy feeling. Just kidding! But how do we keep the flame of enthusiasm alive?

If we live on the surface of life, we will never make it. If we are to keep enthusiasm for our commitments, we have to dig deep within ourselves. We usually think of the "burning,", the enthusiasm as a spontaneous emotion. It is that, and it feels wonderful. However, such spontaneous emotions do not last long. In life, love and enthusiasm must become an act of the will. We are enthused because we decide to be. We love because we choose to. This is not supposed to be easy. Commitments are never easy.

We know that we cannot go through life in a high state of hysteria. We see people who try, and they can be a real trial. I know people who try to be brimming with happiness every single minute. Spare me! That is simply not real. But we can keep some burning going on in our hearts. The love of God does not have to be just another reality we take for granted.

When God comes for us at the hour of our death, may He find us still burning for His Presence.

I
F YOU HAVE READ this far, you have read almost 200 of
my reflections on life. My hope is that they may have
inspired some thought on your part. I do not write as a
teacher, but as a fellow traveler. We all experience life. Life can
make us all wise. Any of us can reflect on life and share our
thoughts with our loved ones. In fact, I think that we all have an
obligation to do so in some way. A younger generation has a right
to expect wisdom from older people. So, I hope my thoughts have
inspired your thoughts.

Years ago, I remember celebrating a home Mass. I was serving in
a campus parish. That living room was filled with college professors,
except for one grandmother from next door. She was from Eastern
Europe, spoke broken English, had no education, and was scared to
death among the professors. She spoke not a word in the discussion.
I later learned that she had more wisdom than anyone there did. We
shut her down with our learning, to our own detriment. What a
shame! Wisdom is like gold; it is where you find it. It can be
anywhere, even in a grandma who is not articulate.

To achieve wisdom, we must drain all that we can from our
human experience. In every experience, we need to ask, "What is God
trying to tell me in this experience?" "What can I learn here?"
There is always a message; there is always something to learn.

I hope the learning, the reflecting, and the sharing go on and on.

T.S. Eliot said it best:

We shall never cease from exploration
And the end of all our exploring
Will be to arrive where we started
And to know that place for the first time.

Acknowledgements

Mary Riedner Baker   James Nelson
Suzanne Bauman   Shirley Springer
Tim Dechant   Lois Werner
Ron Leifeld   Sheila Wood

ABOUT THE AUTHOR

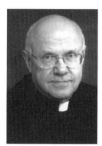

The REVEREND JAMES O'LEARY was born a triplet in 1935 in Lansing, Michigan. He graduated from Sacred Heart Seminary in Detroit and completed postgraduate studies in theology at the Gregorian University in Rome, Italy. He was ordained in St. Peter's Basilica in 1961. Father O'Leary served as an Associate Pastor at Holy Redeemer, Flint; St. Paul, Owosso; St. Augustine, Kalamazoo; and St. Joseph, St. Joseph. Pastorates include Sacred Heart, Bangor; St. Thomas More, Kalamazoo; Holy Angels, Sturgis; St. Charles, Coldwater; and St. Joseph, Battle Creek, Michigan. He has conducted numerous workshops for both the laity and clergy, throughout the Midwest. His ministry has included an outreach to the Hispanic community, the orphaned youth of Mission Honduras, and Alcoholics Anonymous.

This collection is comprised of reflections of Father O'Leary's ministry and life experiences that were originally published in the weekly St. Joseph Parish bulletin. Father O'Leary encourages and inspires all to participate in what he considers life's greatest challenge: The Spiritual Journey.

Proceeds from the sale of this book support the
Battle Creek Area Catholic Schools Foundation.

Additional copies may be purchased by contacting:
The Battle Creek Area Catholic Schools Foundation
63 North 24th Street
Battle Creek, Michigan 49015
(TEL) 269-963-1131 - (FAX) 269-963-3917